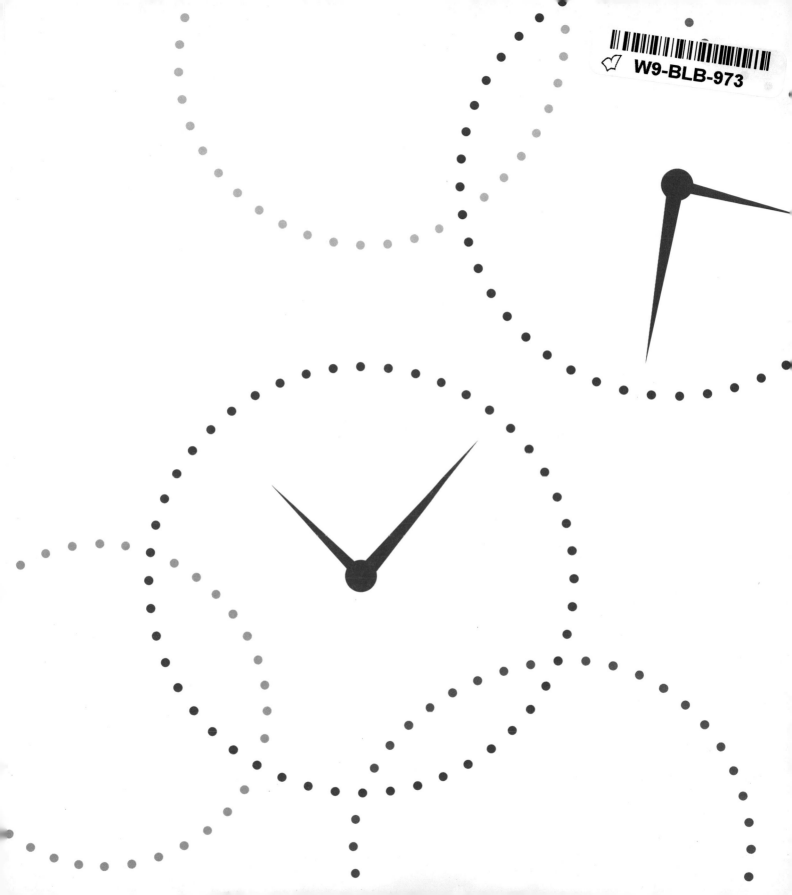

kosher by design
short on time
fabulous food faster

SUSIE FISHBEIN

Photographs by John Uher

Food Styling and Recipe Testing by Melanie Dubberley

Table Décor Design by Renee S. Erreich and Larry Sexton

Graphic Design by Tzini Fruchthandler

Art Direction by Eli Kroen

Published by
Mesorah Publications, ltd

Published by ARTSCROLL / SHAAR PRESS
4401 Second Avenue / Brooklyn, NY 11232 / (718) 921-9000
www.artscroll.com • www.kosherbydesign.com

Distributed in Israel by SIFRIATI / A. GITLER
6 Hayarkon Street / Bnei Brak 51127 / Israel

Distributed in Europe by LEHMANNS
Unit E, Viking Business Park, Rolling Mill Road
Jarrow, Tyne and Wear, NE32 3DP / England

Distributed in Australia and New Zealand by GOLDS WORLD OF JUDAICA
3-13 William Street / Balaclava, Melbourne 3183, Victoria / Australia

Distributed in South Africa by KOLLEL BOOKSHOP
Shop 8A Norwood Hypermarket / Norwood 2196 / Johannesburg, South Africa

ISBN-10: 1-57819-072-X
ISBN-13: 978-1-57819-072-0

Printed in the USA by Noble Book Press

THANK YOU!

To the delicious team of people who come in and out of my life throughout each new book: Damian Sansonetti, Melanie Dubberley, John Uher, Paul Williams, Dan Cronemeyer, Renee Erreich, Larry Sexton, Tzini Fruchthandler, Mary Goodbody, Karen Berman, Felice Eisner, Eli Kroen, Elizabeth Parson and Lorena Barrios. Everything I do is better because of each of you. Thank you for joining me on this adventure.

To Linda and Lenny Spector and Myrna Fishbein, the best PR agents (and parents) in the business.

Thank you to my late father-in-law, Eli Fishbein ע"ה, whose appreciation for fine things, from music to food to all aspects of life, influenced my own life in so many ways.

Thank you to Gedaliah Zlotowitz and the ArtScroll/Mesorah family for giving our readers such beautiful books and for giving me a career doing something I love so much.

To my husband Kalman and our children, Kate, Danielle, Jodi, and Eli; it seems that when I am the shortest on time, you are the longest on love, good humor, and patience. I love you so much and am grateful for each of you every day.

All of my memories of my grandparents ע"ה are happy ones, and so many of them include food.

I can recall romping though my Grandpa Morris Sokol's butcher store on Division Avenue in Williamsburg, Brooklyn, and then sitting on the special stool in his and Grandma Mollie's apartment which overlooked the Williamsburg Bridge. I remember happily eating my grandma's spaghetti and looking forward to dessert, which was the spare chocolate bar that my grandmother always carried in her purse in case of emergency.

A trip to my Bobby Miriam and Grandpa Abe Spector's apartment in Queens always meant standing on my tippy-toes to get to the top, red-velvet-lined drawer in their sideboard. Most people keep their sterling in this drawer, but my grandparents kept the gum, mints, and other treats just for the grandkids.

This book is dedicated in their sweet memories and in their honor.

THE KOSHER KITCHEN

Kosher cooks today have advantages undreamed of by their grandmothers: meat and poultry come from the butcher already koshered; kosher wines have taken top awards in international competitions; and most importantly, thousands upon thousands of food products now have reliable rabbinic supervision — and the number of kosher certified products is constantly growing!

Below is a summary of rules about kosher cooking. If your kitchen is not yet kosher (including your appliances), or if you have questions concerning kosher cooking, contact a qualified rabbi for guidance.

- Meat and dairy are cooked and eaten separately, using separate utensils, including dishes and flatware. The utensils are also washed separately.

- All meat must be slaughtered by trained, certified kosher slaughterers; the blood is then removed in accordance with Jewish law. In many places, the butcher "koshers" the meat (removes the blood) using the prescribed salting and soaking process. If you need to "kosher" your own meat, consult a rabbi (in advance) about the proper procedure.

- Liver is "koshered" by salting and broiling (see note on page 10).

- Foods that are neither meat nor dairy (such as vegetables, eggs, grains) are called parve. They may be eaten with meat or dairy, but to retain their parve status they must be cooked in designated parve utensils.

- Only fish with fins and scales are kosher and do not require special koshering. All other seafood is prohibited. Althogh fish is parve, it may not be eaten together with meat.

- Eggs with bloodspots are discarded.

- All processed food products, including wine and cheese, require kosher certification.

- Produce must be well-washed and checked for insects.

- Passover requires its own set of meat, dairy and parve utensils as well as Passover certified foods.

While these rules may sound complicated, they are not difficult to keep once your kitchen is set up correctly. A well-arranged kosher kitchen just hums along — meat, dairy, and parve dishes and utensils are well marked (usually by color coding). A rabbi's phone number is kept handy for consultation if a mistake occurs. And the cook knows that both family and guests are eating food prepared in accordance with Jewish law, ensuring their spiritual, as well as physical, well being.

CONTENTS

INTRODUCTION

Anyone who has ever walked in the house after a long day to face an empty kitchen and a hungry family knows the dread that I address in this book. As I traveled around the country during the past few years to give cooking demonstrations, I met hundreds of people. Time, or the lack of it, is an issue that so many of them have in common. They want their families to eat well but find that when they are busy, they tend to prepare meals on the fly, or they rely too often on take-out meals.

As a working woman and mother of four, I "get" the need for recipes for everyday life. Sure, there is a place for elaborate dishes, and I understand that many need time and attention to fully develop flavors and cook to perfection. For me, there is no better way to unwind than in my kitchen with music playing and something delicious simmering on my stove. But there is also a time and a place for quick, simple meals that can be thrown together in a matter of minutes and still yield wonderful results, both in terms of flavor and visual appeal. This is the food that I present in this book.

Short on Time is filled with recipes to turn to when you have just minutes to get dinner on the table. It also offers plenty of recipes that demand only a few minutes of your attention and then can be left to cook in the oven or on top of the stove while you tend to other family responsibilities. On these pages, you will find a section of recipes for the slow cooker for those days when you know you will need a warm meal to greet you at the door at the end of the day. There is a section of what I call "building blocks," which are homemade recipes that you can use as the basis for dozens of your own creations. Within this book, you will also discover that many hearty soups and protein-laden salads can stand alone as a whole meal. And I have not forgotten dessert. None are hard or elaborate, but all are homey and deliciously appealing.

Before you begin to cook, read through the recipe so that you know what to anticipate. If pasta needs to be boiled, use that time to dice, chop, or prep the other ingredients that come later in the recipe. If something requires chilling, figure the time in the refrigerator when you make your overall plan. Whenever possible, I have provided tips for what can be prepared ahead of time and what needs reheating.

Accordingly, you will find that you need very few pieces of equipment to make the recipes, although there are a few items that will cut your time in the kitchen and make the experience smoother and more gratifying. These include a good sharp chef's knife and paring knife, sturdy cutting boards, an immersion blender, a slow cooker and a food processor. Most importantly, treat yourself to a

14-inch nonstick skillet. The majority of recipes are for six to eight servings and this size skillet will make preparing many of them easy; you won't have to prepare them in batches as you might with smaller skillets and the pots and pans included in most "cookware sets." When I developed the recipes, I had my family in mind and wanted to create meals with ample leftovers, and so the large pan comes in handy. The best place to find these skillets (and other equipment) is in a housewares store or restaurant supply house. The pans are not rare or difficult to find but I do urge you to buy one. It will get a workout!

Good cooking starts with good ingredients. For the best success, have the basics on hand so that every new recipe does not require a trip to the store. For example, no pantry should be without good-quality olive oil, vegetable oil, roasted sesame oil, balsamic vinegar, cider vinegar, rice vinegar, mirin, taco and fajita seasoning packets, assorted spices, Worcestershire sauce, hot sauce, good-quality preserves, soy sauce and honey. It is also a good idea to keep some bottles of liquor and wine on hand, such as rum, sherry, red wine and white wine. Make sure you always have onions, pre-peeled garlic cloves, and shallots available, too.

Keep your cupboard stocked with assorted canned beans, lentils, jars of roasted red peppers, marinated artichoke hearts, olives, ketchup, rice, pasta, cornmeal, panko breadcrumbs and boxed parve vegetable stock. Baking items should include flour, sugar, pure vanilla extract, Dutch-processed cocoa, Wondra flour, high-quality chocolate, old-fashioned rolled oats and boxes of vanilla and chocolate pudding mix. Finally, parchment paper is a must, as are plastic wrap and aluminum foil.

A kosher refrigerator should hold soy milk, orange juice, nondairy sour cream, nondairy cream cheese, unsalted butter, margarine, and fresh herbs such as flat-leaf parsley and fresh basil. Your freezer should be stocked with good-quality purchased chicken stock, puff pastry, phyllo dough, assorted nuts, nondairy whipping cream and ice cream; both parve and dairy.

Salt and pepper may be the most basic of cooking ingredients, but I think they need a little explanation. Arguably, the biggest difference between restaurant chefs and home cooks is how they use salt and pepper and what kinds they use. Chefs are constantly tasting and seasoning their food and they are apt to rely on freshly ground black or white pepper and fine or coarse sea salt. I have a pretty pepper mill that I happily leave on the countertop so that it's always within an arm's reach. I never use pre-ground pepper but keep big jars of black and white peppercorns in the spice cupboard to stock the mill. I have stopped using both iodized (ordinary table) salt and kosher salt and instead use fine sea salt in place of the former and coarse sea salt in place of the latter. Sea salt adds a multifaceted flavor to food. Sprinkle a little on a plain slice of tomato and sprinkle iodized salt on a second slice. Taste how the sea salt brightens the tomato's flavors so that they come alive. The iodized salt tastes a little flat and metallic. Sea salt is more expensive than table salt, so if cost is a factor, reserve it for sprinkling on top of food before serving. I keep a tray of small decorative salt cellars right by my stove. This way, sea salt, coarse sea salt and the fancy finishing salt, fleur de sel, are just a pinch away. When I call for sea salt in the recipes, I mean fine sea salt, unless otherwise specified.

It helps a lot, too, to have the cooking equipment you need on hand. I organize my utensils so that I can grab them when needed. For instance, I separate measuring spoons and stand them in a pretty mug with other tools such as thin metal spatulas and a melon baller. This way, you can find them instantaneously without pawing through a crowded drawer. (I also recommend you have more than one set of measuring spoons; they are useful when you're baking and measuring different ingredients.) Keep a pretty decanter near the stove for whisks, ladles, tongs, slotted spoons, wooden spoons and assorted silicone spatulas. Don't worry about it looking messy; these are the touches that add personality to the kitchen and turn it into a working one. When you keep them in pretty containers, they will look neat and tidy. I have mine in a brown chintz pitcher so it fits in as a piece of décor.

Speaking of décor, I hope you will enjoy the quick and easy table-decorating ideas. Being short on time doesn't mean you need to be short on style.

Cooking every day when you are short on time can be as satisfying as cooking a complicated dinner party. And it's far easier! Simple, straightforward recipes taste great and with just a little organization and planning, you and your family can enjoy them five, six, seven times a week.

Susie Fishbein

APPETIZERS

chicken liver crostini

Status: Meat

Prep Time: 5 minutes

Cook Time: 5 minutes

Yield: 6–8 servings

1 pound chicken livers, kashered as below, or pre-kashered packaged chicken livers

6-8 (½-inch) slices of French or Italian bread

olive oil

2 cloves fresh garlic, minced

2 shallots, minced

2 tablespoons balsamic vinegar

1 tablespoon chopped fresh flat-leaf Italian parsley

Coarsely chop the chicken livers into bite-sized pieces. Set aside.

Place the sliced bread on a cookie sheet. Drizzle with olive oil. Place under the broiler for 2 minutes to lightly toast the crostini.

Meanwhile, heat 1 tablespoon olive oil in a medium skillet. Add the garlic and shallots and sauté for 2 minutes until fragrant and shiny. Add the livers to the pan, stirring to combine. Swirl in the balsamic vinegar and heat through. Remove from heat. Sprinkle in the chopped parsley.

Spoon 1–2 tablespoons over each crostini.

Chicken livers must be kashered in a specific way. If your butcher does not sell kashered liver, here are directions for kashering raw liver:

Use a sharp knife to poke holes in a disposable broiler pan and set it right into another disposable roasting pan of the same size. After trimming all visible fat from the livers and rinsing them under running water 3 times on each side, salt lightly with kosher (coarse) salt. Place the chicken livers on the broiler pan, and broil until the blood is cooked out, at least five minutes on each side. Rinse livers again under running water, 3 times on each side. Dispose of the pans.

The crostini are great warm or at room temperature and are fine if made a day or two in advance. Keep the crostini in the pantry in a Ziploc bag and the liver in the refrigerator until ready to serve.

cherry chicken puffs

Status: Meat

Prep Time: 15 minutes

Cook Time: 25 minutes

Yield: 6 servings

1½ (1-pound) boxes puff-pastry squares, such as Kineret brand

2 boneless, skinless chicken breast halves, cut into ½-inch dice

6 crimini mushrooms, quartered

2 (15-ounce) cans sweet dark pitted cherries, divided

1 tablespoon cornstarch

3 tablespoons sugar

¼ teaspoon fine sea salt

¼ teaspoon freshly ground black pepper

Preheat oven to 400°F and line a cookie sheet with parchment paper. Allow the puff pastry to stand at room temperature for 15 minutes so that it stretches more easily.

In a medium bowl, toss the chicken cubes and mushrooms. Drain and discard the juice from one can of cherries. Cut each cherry from this can in half and add into the bowl. Set aside.

Place the puff pastry squares on a work surface in a single layer. Spoon one-sixth of the chicken mixture onto the center of each pastry square.

Top each filled square with a second square of puff pastry, enclosing the chicken, cherries, and mushrooms. Use the tines of a fork to decoratively seal each pastry packet.

Place the chicken packets onto the prepared cookie sheet.

Bake for 25 minutes, until the pastry is puffed and golden.

Meanwhile, empty the second can of cherries with its liquid into a medium pot. Add the cornstarch, sugar, salt, and pepper. Bring to a boil. Reduce heat and simmer for 10 minutes until the sauce thickens. Spoon some of the sauce over each chicken puff.

If you can't find puff pastry squares, use 1½ (17.5-ounce) boxes puff pastry, cutting 3 of the sheets into 4 squares each.

seven-layer dip

Status: Dairy

Prep Time: 10 minutes

Cook Time: none

Yield: 8–10 servings

8 ounces store-bought chunky salsa

1 (15-ounce) can refried pinto beans, such as Eden brand

3 tablespoons taco seasoning, from a 1.25-ounce packet, such as Ortega brand

1 (16-ounce) container sour cream, divided

1 (16-ounce) can black beans, drained and rinsed

1 cup store-bought guacamole or avocado mixture as directed in note below

4 ounces shredded cheddar cheese

1 (2.25-ounce) can sliced black olives, drained

tortilla chips

Pour the salsa into a fine-mesh strainer set over a bowl. Press it slightly with the back of a spoon and allow the liquid to drain out.

Empty the can of refried beans into a small bowl. Mix in the taco seasoning and 5 tablespoons sour cream. Stir with a fork to mash and lighten until combined.

Pour the bean mixture into a 9- or 10-inch glass pie plate; spread evenly. Or divide the mixture between 8–10 margarita glasses and spread to even out the tops. Spread with a layer of remaining sour cream.

Add a layer of salsa.

Pile on the black beans.

Spread with a layer of guacamole or avocado mixture.

Top with shredded cheese and sliced olives.

Serve with tortilla chips.

I like the fresh salsas that are sold in the refrigerator case at the supermarket. They are brighter and better-tasting than jarred, although, by all means, a thick jarred salsa can stand in here. Select the heat according to your taste — I like a medium-spicy flavor.

If you cannot find store-bought guacamole, substitute this mixture: 2 ripe Haas avocados, pitted and mashed with 1 teaspoon bottled lime juice, 1 clove minced garlic, 2 finely chopped scallions, 2 tablespoons finely chopped fresh cilantro leaves, and ¼ teaspoon fine sea salt.

pesto-glazed orzo, salmon, and artichokes

Status: Parve

Prep Time: 15 minutes

Cook Time: 25 minutes

Yield: 6–8 servings

1½ pounds salmon fillet, all pinbones removed

fine and coarse sea salts

freshly ground black pepper

12 whole button mushrooms, cleaned and halved

4 tablespoons olive oil, divided

1 (1-pound) box orzo

1 bunch basil (2 cups packed leaves)

¼ cup raw, shelled pistachios, not roasted or salted

1 cup extra-virgin olive oil

1 (6-ounce) jar marinated artichoke hearts, drained

Preheat oven to 375°F. Spray a broiler pan with nonstick cooking spray.

Place the salmon on the broiler pan. Season with fine sea salt and pepper.

Toss the mushrooms with 1 tablespoon olive oil. Arrange them around the salmon.

Roast for 25 minutes. Set aside.

Meanwhile, place remaining 3 tablespoons of olive oil into a large soup pot over medium heat. Add orzo and stir to coat with warm oil. Toast until lightly browned and fragrant, stirring occasionally.

Add water to come up halfway on the pot. Add 2 tablespoons fine or coarse sea salt and bring to a boil. Cook orzo until tender, usually 9–11 minutes. Drain and rinse orzo and set aside in a medium bowl.

Place basil leaves into a quart-sized or other high-sided container. Add pistachios, 1 cup extra-virgin olive oil, and a pinch of fine sea salt. Using an immersion blender, purée the mixture. This can also be done in a food processor.

Pour half of this pesto into the orzo. Break the salmon into chunks and add it to the orzo. Add the mushrooms and artichokes. Season with ½ teaspoon fine sea salt. Toss to combine.

Place into a bowl or serving platter and drizzle with remaining pesto.

Best served warm or at room temperature.

This dish comes up often in my cooking line-up after a simple salmon dinner. It is a great way to add new flavor and create a total make-over for leftover salmon. You can serve it in larger portions as a main dish or as a take-along to a picnic.

salami quiche florentine

Status: Meat

Prep Time: 15 minutes

Cook Time: 20 minutes

Yield: 12 mini tarts
or 1 (9-inch) tart

4 large eggs

½ cup soy milk

 pinch of cayenne pepper

¼ teaspoon fine sea salt

1 tablespoon olive oil

½ red onion, minced

½ cup packed baby spinach leaves, coarsely chopped

12 small (3-inch diameter) pastry shells or 1 (9-inch) tart shell, defrosted

3-4 tablespoons yellow mustard

4 ounces salami (from a whole salami, not slices)

Preheat oven to 375°F.

In a medium bowl, whisk the eggs, soy milk, cayenne pepper, and salt. Set aside.

Heat the olive oil in a medium skillet over medium heat. Add the red onion and sauté for 3–4 minutes until it is shiny and translucent.

Whisk the onions and spinach into the eggs.

Brush the tart shells with a thin coating of mustard. Cut the salami into ¼-inch cubes. Place a small pile of salami cubes into each mini tart shell or all over the bottom of the larger tart.

With a ladle, pour the egg and spinach mixture into the tart shells. You may have a little extra.

Place the tart shells on a cookie sheet to catch any drips and bake for 20 minutes, until the eggs are set and puffy.

Serve hot or at room temperature.

When I was a kid, one of my mom's quick and easy dinners was salami and eggs. Here is a prettier version served as individual quiches with added color and nutrients from the baby spinach.

sausage en croûte

Status: Meat

Prep Time: 10 minutes

Cook Time: 25 minutes

Yield: 6 servings

1 (17.5-ounce) box frozen puff-pastry dough

1 large egg, lightly beaten

1 tablespoon Dijon mustard

6 brown-and-serve sausages, such as 999 brand fully-cooked Italian or Beef Sausage

yellow mustard

Preheat oven to 400°F and line a cookie sheet with parchment paper. Allow the puff pastry to stand at room temperature for 15 minutes so that it stretches easily.

Gently open each sheet of puff pastry.

Lightly brush beaten egg over the surface of each sheet.

Lightly brush Dijon mustard over the surface of each sheet.

Cut each puff pastry sheet lengthwise into 3 equal pieces, using the folds as guidelines.

Place a sausage in the center of each piece. Wrap the pastry around each sausage. Pinch the ends closed and trim as necessary.

Place the sausages on the prepared cookie sheet.

Bake for 20–25 minutes until the pastry is puffed and golden.

Serve with yellow mustard.

When I was in HAFTR High School, a group of my friends and I worked as hostesses for the caterer whose hall was right next door to our school. My favorite part of the job was serving hors d'oeuvres. I was continually amazed that no matter how many fabulous and exotic appetizers were passed around, the basket that got the most attention was filled with the franks-in-blankets. They always disappeared immediately. This recipe is a spicy, more contemporary version, but just as simple to make.

The puff pastry can be filled and rolled up to 1 day in advance and refrigerated, or frozen up to 2 weeks in advance. Thaw and bake as directed. You can serve a whole sausage as an appetizer portion, or slice them up and arrange them on a platter as hors d'oeuvres.

steamed artichokes with two sauces

Status: Dairy or Parve

Prep Time: 10 minutes

Cook Time: 35 minutes

Yield: 6 servings

1 lemon

6 large fresh whole artichokes, or 12 baby artichokes

fine sea salt

freshly ground black pepper

LEMON-CHIVE SAUCE:

½ cup (1 stick) butter or margarine, melted

1 tablespoon fresh lemon juice

1 teaspoon lemon zest

2 chives, finely chopped

BALSAMIC VINAIGRETTE:

½ cup extra-virgin olive oil

¼ cup balsamic vinegar

2 cloves fresh garlic, minced

1 tablespoon chopped fresh parsley

Fill a large bowl with water and the juice of the lemon.

Slice the stem from each artichoke to form a flat base so the artichoke can stand upright on a plate. Discard the stem. While working with one artichoke, place the others in the bowl of lemon water to prevent them from discoloring.

Holding it on its side, cut off the top third of the artichoke. Pull back the outer leaves until they break at the base. Stop when you get to the pale green layers. Repeat with remaining artichokes.

Place 2 inches of water in the bottom of a large pot and add 1 teaspoon salt. Stand the artichokes in the pot. Cover and place the pot over medium heat. Steam the artichokes until one of the leaves pulls off easily, about 25–35 minutes, depending on size. Drain and serve with choice of sauce. Remind your guests to discard the fuzzy choke before they enjoy the tender heart.

LEMON CHIVE SAUCE: In a medium bowl, whisk the melted butter or margarine with the lemon juice, zest, and chives. Season with salt and black pepper.

BALSAMIC VINAIGRETTE: In a medium bowl, whisk the olive oil, balsamic, garlic, and parsley. Season with salt and black pepper.

Artichokes may look strange, but they are fun to eat. The traditional way to eat steamed artichokes is to pull off one leaf at a time and scrape the tender meat from the lower edge of the leaf with your teeth. When all of the leaves are off, your guests scoop out the fuzzy choke with a spoon and discard it. They are left with the "heart," the really delicious flavorful center.

Artichokes are great by themselves but a dipping sauce adds extra flavor. When you are really short on time, bottled Italian dressing is a great accompaniment. When you have time, you may want to trim thorny tips off the outer leaves with kitchen shears.

creamy chummos with steeped tomatoes

Status: Parve

Prep Time: 10 minutes

Cook Time: none

Needs chill time

Yield: 8–10 servings

1 (15-ounce) can small white beans or cannellini beans, drained and rinsed

1 (15-ounce) can chickpeas (garbanzo beans), drained and rinsed

3 cloves fresh garlic

½ cup tahini (also called sesame paste)

juice of 2 lemons

1½ tablespoons soy sauce

1½ teaspoons fine sea salt

1½ teaspoons ground cumin

½ teaspoon cayenne pepper

⅛ teaspoon ground white pepper

⅓ cup extra-virgin olive oil

¼ cup cold water or more as needed

STEEPED TOMATOES:

2 plum tomatoes

1 clove fresh garlic, minced

¼ cup fresh basil, minced

extra-virgin olive oil

8-10 large pita breads, warmed in the oven, cut into triangles

Place beans, chickpeas, garlic, tahini, lemon juice, soy sauce, salt, cumin, cayenne pepper, and white pepper into the bowl of a food processor fitted with a metal blade. Process for 1 minute.

Drizzle in ⅓ cup olive oil and water. Process again. Add more water as needed to thin the chummos to desired consistency.

Transfer the chummos to a plastic or glass container; cover and chill in the refrigerator.

Cut each tomato in half and discard the seeds and juices. Chop the halves into small dice, place into a small bowl and add the garlic, basil, and olive oil to cover. Cover the bowl and place it into the refrigerator to give the flavors a chance to steep.

To serve, top chummos with steeped tomatoes. Serve with warm pita bread.

Chummos, also known as hummus, is a real Middle Eastern specialty. It is served in every home, restaurant, market, and food stand in Israel. My Israeli cousin whips up a fresh batch for almost every meal. There are countless recipes that include add-ins of all sorts, from capers to roasted red peppers. This recipe provides fiber and a velvety texture with a can of white beans, and a special splash of color with its steeped-tomato garnish. Both parts can be made up to three days in advance.

Kosher by Design Short on Time

moroccan meat turnovers

Status: Meat

Prep Time: 20 minutes

Cook Time: 25 minutes

Yield: 8 servings

1 large egg

2 tablespoons olive oil

½ onion, finely chopped

1 clove fresh garlic, coarsely chopped

1 large tomato, chopped

1 tablespoon tomato paste

½ pound ground beef or ground lamb

1 clove fresh garlic, minced

1 tablespoon chopped fresh parsley

¼ teaspoon ground cumin

¼ teaspoon paprika

¼ teaspoon ground cinnamon

¼ teaspoon cayenne pepper

¼ teaspoon fine sea salt

¼ teaspoon freshly ground black pepper

pinch of ground ginger

1 (1-pound) box puff-pastry dough squares, or 1 (17.5-ounce) box puff-pastry sheets, cut into 8 squares, thawed

sesame seeds

store-bought or homemade chummos (see page 24), optional

Preheat oven to 400°F. Line a cookie sheet with parchment paper; set aside.

In a small bowl, lightly beat the egg with 1 tablespoon water. Set aside.

Heat the oil in a large skillet over medium heat. Add the onion and cook for 4–5 minutes, until shiny. Add the chopped garlic, chopped tomato, and tomato paste. Sauté for 3 minutes.

Meanwhile, in a medium bowl, combine the ground meat, minced garlic, parsley, cumin, paprika, cinnamon, cayenne pepper, salt, pepper, and ginger. Mix well to distribute the spices evenly.

Add the meat mixture to the pan. Sauté for 3–4 minutes or until liquid evaporates and meat is cooked through.

On a sheet of parchment paper, slightly roll out each puff pastry square. Spoon 1–2 heaping tablespoons of meat mixture into the center of each square, leaving a border of pastry. Brush edges of the square with egg mixture. Fold squares to form triangles. Using the tines of a fork, press edges to seal. Place 2 inches apart on prepared cookie sheet. Brush with egg mixture and sprinkle with sesame seeds.

Bake for 25 minutes, until the pastry is puffed and golden. Serve each turnover with a dollop of chummos if desired.

Just the aromas that escape from these meat turnovers when you cut them open make the small amount of effort well worth it. Who can resist the heady mingling of cumin, cinnamon, garlic, and sesame seeds?

hoisin-glazed turkey timbales

Status: Meat

Prep Time: 10 minutes

Cook Time: 25 minutes

Yield: 12 turkey timbales

1 cup bottled hoisin sauce, such as Joyce Chen brand

½ cup orange juice, or the juice from 2 navel oranges

2 teaspoons roasted or toasted sesame oil

1 pound ground dark meat turkey

1 pound ground white meat turkey

2 cloves fresh garlic, minced

1 teaspoon onion powder

1 teaspoon ground ginger

1 teaspoon hot sauce, such as Tabasco

½ teaspoon freshly ground black pepper

⅓ cup soy sauce

Preheat oven to 375°F. Spray a 12-cup muffin tin with nonstick cooking spray. Set aside.

In a small pot, mix hoisin sauce, orange juice, and sesame oil. Set aside.

In a large mixing bowl, combine both types of ground turkey, garlic, onion powder, ginger, hot sauce, black pepper, and soy sauce. Mix very well to distribute all the ingredients evenly.

Separate mixture into 12 equal portions. Place one portion into each muffin cup, press to flatten. Depress the center slightly more than the outer edges.

Remove ¼ cup of the glaze to use for basting the raw turkey timbales, reserving the rest to use as a glaze after cooking. Brush the tops of each timbale, using the ¼ cup of the hoisin glaze.

Place the turkey timbales into the oven for 25 minutes. Re-warm the remaining glaze.

Serve each turkey loaf with some of the warm hoisin glaze.

Ground turkey is a very healthy, low-fat protein. Turkey tends to have a mild flavor, so it really benefits from added spice like in this recipe.

tri colore salad pizza

Status: Parve

Prep Time: 10 minutes

Cook Time: 20 minutes

Yield: 6 servings

3 (1-pound) balls pizza dough

extra-virgin olive oil

coarse sea salt

freshly ground black pepper

6 cloves fresh garlic, minced

⅓ cup plus 1 tablespoon balsamic vinegar, such as the Bartenura Special Reserve

½ cup extra-virgin olive oil

1 teaspoon dried oregano

2 large handfuls arugula

2 large handfuls radicchio

2 large handfuls red leaf lettuce

3 plum tomatoes, thinly sliced

Preheat oven to 400°F. Cover 2–3 large cookie sheets with parchment paper. Set aside.

Cut each dough ball in half. Knead and work each half into a flattened round, like a mini pizza crust, about 7 inches in diameter. Place each round onto the prepared cookie sheets.

Brush each crust with olive oil. Sprinkle each with coarse sea salt and pepper. Divide the garlic evenly over the crusts. Use your fingers to spread the minced garlic evenly.

Place the cookie sheets into the oven and bake the crusts for 20 minutes.

Meanwhile, place the balsamic into a microwave-safe dish. Microwave for 45–60 seconds. The smell will be pungent and the vinegar will boil and steam. Reducing the vinegar results in a much richer flavor.

Whisk the oil into the reduced vinegar. Add the oregano. Set aside.

Shred the lettuces and toss them together. Thinly slice the tomatoes.

When the crusts are done, remove them from the oven. Place some of the lettuce mix on each crust, leaving a narrow rim. Scatter tomato slices in the center of each crust.

Whisk the dressing again and drizzle each pizza with the vinaigrette.

My sister Karen loves good food as much as I do, and she is pretty health conscious. On a recent visit she ordered in from her local pizza store and surprised me with a fabulous find that inspired this recipe — a salad pizza.

The pizza dough that I like comes in plastic bags in the freezer section of my supermarket. I always keep a few balls on hand for last minute make-your-own pizza nights or for this, a really colorful, flavorful, healthier alternative. Some stores, like Trader Joe's, sell fresh dough balls in the refrigerator section in similar plastic bags, or you can purchase them from your local pizza store.

chili bites

Status: Dairy or Parve

Prep Time: 5 minutes

Cook Time: 5 minutes

Yield: 15 chili cups

1 (2.1-ounce) box mini phyllo (fillo) cups, such as Athens brand

1 (10-ounce) bag Lightlife Smart Chili

½ cup dairy or nondairy sour cream

paprika

Preheat oven to 350°F. Place the phyllo cups on a parchment-lined cookie sheet; no need to thaw them.

Bake for 3–5 minutes.

Meanwhile, heat the chili in the microwave according to package directions, or in a small pot over medium heat.

Fill each cup with chili. Top with a small dollop of sour cream.

Sprinkle with paprika.

If Martha Stewart and Ina Garten had collaborated on building and decorating a house, it would be Tranquility Bay. This incredible home on the water actually belongs to Elanna Rosenbaum, who was my gracious hostess for a cooking demonstration that I did for her school, Sha'arei Bina, in Miami, Florida. We spent many hours prepping side by side in her gorgeous kitchen. As we cooked, we joked about how we Jews over-plan and over-serve our meals all the while we were adding dips, various hors d'oeuvres, and crudites to our menu for the evening. I was about to draw the line when Elanna described the following recipe, which I fell in love with. The chili is brand-specific; it is made of vegetable protein and beans. It is so outstanding and healthy it is worth tracking down. Whole Foods and other upscale stores carry it. It is in the refrigerator section and is sold in small white bags.

mexicotti

Status: Meat
Prep Time: 15 minutes
Cook Time: 35 minutes
Yield: 6 servings

12 manicotti pasta tubes, uncooked

16 ounces store-bought salsa

1 (26-ounce) jar favorite marinara sauce

1 jalapeño pepper, minced, divided

1½ pounds ground beef

½ cup crushed tortilla chips

⅓ cup fresh cilantro leaves, chopped

½ large green bell pepper, seeded and finely chopped

2 cloves fresh garlic, minced

½ teaspoon fine sea salt

¼ teaspoon freshly ground black pepper

1 small onion, halved and very thinly sliced

nondairy sour cream, such as Tofutti brand, for garnish

lime slices, for garnish

Preheat oven to 375°F. Spray an 8- by 10-inch baking pan with nonstick cooking spray.

Cook the pasta in a large pot of boiling, salted water for half the recommended time on the box. Rinse, drain, cover, and set aside.

Meanwhile, combine the salsa, marinara sauce, and half the minced jalapeño pepper. Set aside.

In a medium bowl, combine the ground beef, crushed tortilla chips, cilantro, green bell pepper, garlic, salt, black pepper, and remaining half of the minced jalapeño pepper. Add ⅔ cup of the prepared salsa mixture. Use your hands to thoroughly mix and knead the mixture together.

With a small spoon, fill the manicotti tubes with the meat mixture; do not overstuff or they will split. Lay the stuffed manicotti into the prepared pan. Mix the onion slices into the remaining sauce. Ladle the sauce over the manicotti.

Bake for 35 minutes, uncovered. Serve 2 Mexicotti per plate with a dollop of nondairy sour cream and a lime slice.

Manicotti is an Italian dish of meat- or cheese-stuffed pasta tubes. This version introduces Mexican flavors. Prepare the meat mixture while the pasta is cooking. You want to undercook the pasta so that it is pliable but doesn't split when you stuff and bake it.

Wear gloves when cutting the jalapeño pepper to keep the capsaicin off your skin, and discard the seeds and ribs. Don't touch eyes or other sensitive areas until your gloves are discarded and your hands are completely clean.

moo shu

Status: Meat

Prep Time: 10 minutes

Cook Time: 15 minutes

Yield: 6 servings

1 tablespoon canola oil

1½ pounds top of the rib, filet split, or London broil, very thinly sliced against the grain

6 ounces shiitake mushrooms caps, thinly sliced

3 scallions, sliced thinly on a diagonal, white and pale green parts only

2 tablespoons soy sauce

2 teaspoons roasted or toasted sesame oil

½ teaspoon ground ginger

¼ teaspoon cayenne pepper

2 large eggs, lightly beaten

bottled hoisin sauce, such as Joyce Chen brand

6 large flour tortillas

In a large skillet or wok, heat the oil over medium heat. Add the slices of steak and mushrooms and sear them for 3 minutes. Turn them over and sear on the other side. Do this in batches, if necessary, to avoid crowding the pan. Add the scallions; sauté for 3 minutes until shiny.

In a small bowl, mix the soy sauce, sesame oil, ginger, and cayenne pepper. Add this mixture to the skillet.

Add the beaten eggs and mix, stirring quickly until partially set. Remove from heat.

Warm the flour tortillas in a microwave for 10 seconds to soften them. You can also do this in the oven; just spritz with a tiny bit of water, wrap in foil, and bake for 5–6 minutes until warm.

Spread each tortilla with hoisin sauce. Fill each with the moo shu mixture. Fold each tortilla in half and then fold into quarters.

Usually wrapped in a thin, delicate Mandarin pancake, my quick and easy version of Moo Shu wraps the filling in warmed flour tortillas, making the preparation a snap.

This recipe can be made with sliced chicken breast as well, or, for a vegetarian spin, substitute raw coleslaw mix for the protein. This dish is perfect for a packed lunch, since it is easy to transport. Think of all the fun you can have just saying Moo Shu...

quesadillas

Status: Dairy

Prep Time: 10 minutes

Cook Time: 7 minutes

Yield: 6 servings

PICO DE GALLO:

- 3 plum tomatoes
- ½ jalapeño pepper, seeds and ribs removed, finely minced
- ½ small onion, cut into ¼-inch dice
- 2 tablespoons chopped cilantro leaves

juice of 1 lime or 1 tablespoon bottled lime juice

fine sea salt

freshly ground black pepper

- 3 scallions, very thinly sliced on a diagonal, for garnish

QUESADILLAS:

- 12 large flour tortillas
- 8-12 ounces shredded cheddar cheese
- 8-12 ounces shredded mozzarella cheese

Monterey Jack cheese, optional

Preheat oven to 400°F. Line 2 large cookie sheets with parchment paper.

In a medium bowl prepare the Pico de Gallo: Cut each tomato in half and discard the seeds and juices. Chop into ¼-inch dice. Toss the tomatoes, jalapeño, onion, cilantro leaves, and lime juice. Mix well. Season with salt and black pepper. Set aside.

Lay 6 of the tortillas on prepared pans in single layers. Sprinkle each tortilla with a layer of cheddar cheese, leaving a small rim around the edge of each one. Top with a layer of mozzarella. Top each with a second tortilla.

Sprinkle a small pile of cheese in the center of the top tortillas. You can even make this a third kind of cheese, such as Monterey Jack cheese.

Bake for 5–7 minutes, until edges are slightly golden and the cheese is melted.

Remove from oven, slice into wedges, and garnish with sliced scallions and pico de gallo. Serve hot.

Quesadillas are the Mexican equivalent of a grilled cheese sandwich. You can add almost anything to it before cooking. Try pan-seared mushrooms, grilled vegetables, olive, tomato slices, really anything can go into it. You can also garnish them with sour cream.

Pico de gallo is a fresh salsa. It is wonderful with these quesadillas but be sure to make extra. It is great on fish or seared chicken cutlets.

avocado or chicken egg rolls

Status: Meat or Parve

Prep Time: 15 minutes

Cook Time: 10 minutes

Yield: 12 egg rolls

CHICKEN EGG ROLLS:

peanut or canola oil

12 egg roll wrappers

2 boneless, skinless chicken breast halves

fine sea salt

freshly ground black pepper

2 tablespoons olive oil

1 red bell pepper, seeded and thinly sliced into 3-inch strips

6 leaves Napa cabbage, shredded

24-36 fresh cilantro leaves

24 fresh mint leaves

AVOCADO EGG ROLLS:

peanut or canola oil

12 egg roll wrappers

1½ Haas avocados, halved and pitted

½ red onion, thinly sliced

24 fresh cilantro leaves

12 large or 24 small fresh basil leaves

cayenne pepper

HOISIN-LIME DIPPING SAUCE:

¼ cup hoisin sauce

2 teaspoons lime juice

¼ teaspoon cayenne pepper

Preheat the oil in a medium pot: Fill the pot halfway with peanut or canola oil. Bring oil to 350°F over medium heat; this usually takes about 10 minutes.

Lay the egg roll wrappers on the diagonal in a single layer.

For chicken egg rolls: slice each breast into 12 thin strips, each 3 inches long. Season with salt and pepper. Heat olive oil in a small skillet over medium heat. Sauté strips for 2 minutes. Center 2 strips each of red bell pepper and chicken horizontally on each wrapper. Top with a generous tablespoon of Napa cabbage, 2–3 cilantro leaves and 2 mint leaves.

For avocado egg rolls: Slice each avocado half lengthwise into 4 slices, remove the skin from each slice. You can reserve the extra avocado half to be a container for the dipping sauce or for another use. Center 1 avocado slice horizontally on each wrapper. Top with a few strips of red onion, 2 cilantro leaves, and 1 large (or 2 small) basil leaves. Sprinkle with a small pinch of cayenne pepper.

The dipping sauce for these egg rolls can be made in advance, but, in a pinch, duck sauce stands in fine. Egg roll and wonton wrappers are sold in most supermarkets in the produce section where the Asian vegetables, cabbages, and tofu are found.

To seal the eggrolls: Brush the edges of each wrapper with water. Fold the nearest corner over filling. Fold the 2 sides over the center. Tightly roll towards the remaining edge; press to seal. Wet and press the corners as necessary to keep it sealed.

Test the oil: Use a thermometer or dip a spare wrapper or a corner of an egg roll into the oil; it should bubble vigorously but not burn. The wrappers should be golden and crispy. Fry the egg rolls in batches for 1–2 minutes, until crisp and golden. Drain on paper towels. Return the oil to 350°F between batches.

Meanwhile prepare the dipping sauce: In a small bowl, mix the hoisin sauce, lime juice, and cayenne pepper. Serve the egg rolls hot with dipping sauce.

breaded mushrooms

Status: Parve

Prep Time: 10 minutes

Cook Time: 10 minutes

Yield: 6 servings

canola oil

3 large eggs

1 cup all-purpose flour

½ teaspoon fine sea salt

⅛ teaspoon freshly ground black pepper

1 cup seasoned bread crumbs

1 large package button mushrooms, cleaned

jarred marinara sauce, warmed

Fill a small pot with 3 inches of canola oil. Heat on medium heat, until temperature reaches 350°F.

Meanwhile, whisk the eggs in a small bowl and set aside.

Mix the flour, salt, and pepper in a separate small bowl.

Pour the bread crumbs into a third bowl.

Working with a few mushrooms at a time, place them into the flour mixture. Toss until evenly coated, shaking off excess.

Place the mushrooms into the beaten eggs. Shake to coat evenly.

Place mushrooms into the bread crumbs and toss to coat evenly. Set aside.

Continue until all the mushrooms have been breaded.

Using a slotted spoon, lower the mushrooms, a few at a time, into the hot oil and cook for 2 minutes, until they are evenly cooked and golden-brown. Drain on paper towels. This may be done in batches.

Serve hot with warm sauce.

You can bread these mushrooms and keep them in the refrigerator for 3–4 days or even in the freezer for up to a month. You can cook them in the hot oil right from there. The temperature of the oil is vital. If it is too hot, the mushrooms will burn on contact but if it is not hot enough they will just soak up the oil. Use a digital thermometer that measures over 350°F or a candy thermometer.

SOUPS

caramelized parsnip carrot soup

Status: Meat, Dairy, or Parve

Prep Time: 10 minutes

Cook Time: 30 minutes

Yield: 8 servings

2 tablespoons margarine

½ medium onion, sliced

2 cloves fresh garlic, coarsely chopped

2 large shallots, sliced

3 parsnips, peeled and thinly sliced

12 ounces packaged grated carrots

2 tablespoons pure maple syrup

1 tablespoon dark-brown sugar

1 teaspoon dried thyme

zest and juice of 1 navel orange

½ teaspoon coarse sea salt

6 cups chicken or vegetable stock

1 cup dairy sour cream or nondairy sour cream, such as the Toffuti brand, for garnish

1 cup fresh parsley, stems discarded, for garnish

Melt the margarine in a large pot over medium heat. Add the onion, garlic, shallots, parsnips, carrots, maple syrup, and brown sugar. Stir to combine.

Allow the vegetable mixture to cook and caramelize for 12–15 minutes, until shiny and browned. Stir to keep the grated carrots from burning. Lower the heat if necessary.

Add the thyme, zest and juice from the orange, salt, and stock. Cover the pot and cook for 10–15 minutes, until the vegetables are fork-tender.

Uncover the pot, and, with an immersion blender, purée the soup until completely smooth. This can also be done by transferring the soup to a blender in batches.

To make the garnish, place the sour cream and the parsley into a quart-sized container. With the immersion blender, purée until the cream becomes light green in color. This can also be done in a food processor fitted with a metal blade or in batches in a blender.

Ladle the soup into bowls. Garnish each bowl with a dollop of the parsley cream.

Grated carrot is sold in bags in supermarkets in the salad section, usually near the coleslaw mix and bags of shredded purple cabbage. It is a convenience and cuts down on the cooking time. If you don't have them, use 12 ounces of baby carrots or thinly sliced carrots; it will just take a little longer to cook.

lentil barley soup

Status: Meat or Parve

Prep Time: 15 minutes

Cook Time: 55 minutes

Yield: 8–10 servings

3 tablespoons olive oil

1 large onion, cut into ¼-inch dice

2 cloves fresh garlic, coarsely chopped

2 carrots, cut into ¼-inch dice

2 stalks celery, cut into ¼-inch dice

1 teaspoon dried oregano

1 teaspoon dried basil

1 teaspoon dried thyme

1 (28-ounce) can diced tomatoes

1 (10-ounce) box frozen chopped spinach

½ cup dried red lentils

½ cup dried green lentils

¼ cup dried pearl barley

8 cups chicken or vegetable stock, plus more for thinning

fine sea salt

freshly ground black pepper

Heat the oil in a large pot over medium heat. Add the onion and garlic, and cook for 3–4 minutes, until shiny and translucent. If they begin to brown, reduce the heat.

Add the carrots, celery, oregano, basil, and thyme. Stir and cook for 3 minutes.

Add the tomatoes and frozen spinach. Stir, although the spinach will be in a solid block; it will defrost and separate as the soup cooks.

Add the red lentils, green lentils, and barley. Add stock.

Cover the pot and simmer over low heat for 45 minutes. Thin with extra stock as needed. If you have no more stock, you can use bouillon powder dissolved in water. Taste and season with salt and pepper as needed.

Ladle into bowls.

This hearty recipe yields a big batch of soup. Plan to serve it over a few meals to make your life easier. The soup just gets better as it sits in the refrigerator, and while the lentils will absorb some of the liquid, you can replenish it with additional stock. Keep extra stock on hand just for this — although water will work too.

creamy thai sweet potato soup

Status: Meat or Parve

Prep Time: 5 minutes

Cook Time: 15 minutes

Yield: 6 servings

1 tablespoon olive oil

2 shallots, thinly sliced

1 (40-ounce) can sweet potatoes, drained

1 cup coconut milk, NOT cream of coconut

5 cups chicken or vegetable stock

1½ tablespoons teriyaki sauce

½ teaspoon hot sauce, such as Tabasco

juice of 1 lime

fine sea salt

chive blossoms or whole chives, for garnish

Heat the oil in a large pot over medium heat. Add the shallots and cook for 3–4 minutes until shiny and translucent. If they start to brown, lower the heat.

Add the sweet potatoes, coconut milk, and stock. Bring to a simmer.

Using an immersion blender right in the pot, purée the soup until smooth. Mix in the teriyaki sauce, hot sauce, and lime juice. Add salt to taste. Simmer for 5 minutes.

Ladle into bowls. Garnish each bowl with 2 chive blossoms or chives.

You can use fresh sweet potatoes if you have the time to bake them or have leftovers from another meal. To bake fresh ones, wrap them in foil and bake at 375°F until they are soft. Peel the potatoes and mash the orange flesh. Use 2 cups of the mash for this soup; if you have any left over, save it for another meal as a side dish.

black-bean soup

Status: Meat

Prep Time: 15 minutes

Cook Time: 20 minutes

Yield: 6 servings

1 tablespoon canola oil

1 rib celery, cut into ½-inch dice

1 onion, cut into ½-inch dice

2 cloves fresh garlic, minced

1 heaping tablespoon tomato paste

1 cup white wine

1 beefsteak tomato, seeded and cut into ½-inch dice

CRISPY TORTILLA STRIPS:

2 flour tortillas, cut in half, and sliced into thin strips

canola oil

2 (15-ounce) cans black beans, drained and rinsed

2 links brown-and-serve (fully cooked) sausage or 3 inches from a salami, cut into ½-inch dice

½ teaspoon dried oregano

4 cups chicken stock

store-bought salsa

fine sea salt

Heat the canola oil in a large soup pot over medium heat. Add the celery and onion and sauté for 3 minutes or until vegetables begin to soften. Add the garlic and tomato paste and sauté for 2 minutes longer. Add the wine, tomato, beans, and sausage. Sprinkle in the oregano.

Add the chicken stock and simmer for 15 minutes.

Ladle into bowls and garnish each bowl with a dollop of salsa.

While the soup is cooking, prepare the tortilla strips: Fill a small skillet halfway with oil. Over medium heat, bring the oil to 350°F; the oil should be very hot but not smoking. Add a tortilla strip; it should bubble. If it doesn't, your oil is not hot enough. Add the strips and fry for 1–2 minutes until crisp and golden. Remove to paper towels, lightly sprinkle with salt. These can be made in advance and kept in a Ziploc bag for 5–7 days. Serve the soup with the tortilla strips.

This soup is really an entire meal in a bowl. I love it as, is but if you like your black-bean soup creamy, purée half the beans with an immersion blender or food processor before adding them.

The sausage that I like best for this dish is Italian Veal and Beef Brown-and-Serve from 999 or International. You can find them in any good kosher supermarket or in the kosher aisle in a well-stocked regular market. You can select a sweeter variety but I love the kick the spicy ones give the soup. Make sure the sausages are the fully cooked variety. If you purchase raw sausages from the butcher, cook them first.

creamy tuscan white-bean soup

Status: Meat, Dairy, or Parve

Prep Time: 10 minutes

Cook Time: 20 minutes

Yield: 8 servings

2 tablespoons olive oil

1 large onion, cut into ¼-inch dice

4 cloves fresh garlic, sliced

½ teaspoon dried thyme

1 teaspoon ground coriander

½ teaspoon ground cumin

½ teaspoon cayenne pepper

4 (15-ounce) cans small white beans or cannellini beans, drained and rinsed

6 cups water or chicken stock

2 teaspoons dry sherry or cooking sherry

fine sea salt

4 tablespoons (½ stick) margarine or butter

fresh parsley or fresh chives, chopped, for garnish

Heat the oil in a large pot over medium heat. Add the onion and cook until translucent and shiny, about 3 minutes. Add the garlic and thyme. Cook for 2 minutes.

Add the coriander, cumin, and cayenne pepper. Allow the spices to cook for 1 minute and begin to toast; they will be aromatic.

Add the beans, water or stock, sherry, and 2 teaspoons salt.

Using an immersion blender right in the pot, purée the soup until smooth. Cook the soup for 10 minutes longer to allow the flavors to develop. Whisk in the margarine or butter.

Taste and season with more salt if necessary.

Ladle into bowls. Garnish with parsley or chopped chives.

This satisfying soup will make you feel as though you are in a sunny Tuscan farmhouse kitchen. Open a bottle of Italian wine, break open a loaf of crusty bread, and sit back and enjoy the experience. No harm in dreaming!

asian big bowl

Status: Meat

Prep Time: 5 minutes

Cook Time: 10 minutes

Yield: 6 servings

½ small head Napa cabbage, about ¾ pound

1 very small head bok choy

8 cups chicken stock

2 boneless, skinless chicken breast halves, sliced into very thin strips

¼ cup grated or shredded carrot

1 (2.8-ounce) packet ramen noodles (discard the seasoning packet)

1 tablespoon mirin rice cooking wine

2 tablespoons soy sauce

3 scallions, sliced very thin on the diagonal, for garnish

Thinly slice the cabbage and bok choy. Set aside.

Pour the chicken stock into a medium pot and bring to a simmer over medium heat. Add the chicken, carrots, cabbage, and bok choy. Simmer for 5 minutes.

Add the ramen noodles and cook for 2 minutes. Remove from heat and stir in the mirin and the soy sauce.

Ladle into bowls. Garnish each bowl with a small handful of sliced scallions.

What do you get when you cross Asian vegetables with old-fashioned chicken soup? A nouveau twist on the traditional. A full meal in a bowl that will warm and satisfy you with its flavors, textures, and healthful qualities. When I tested this soup on my friend Arnie Stein, he gave it the best compliment… "Wow, this tastes like it has MSG!!"

If you need to prepare this dish in advance, don't add the ramen noodles until two minutes before actual serving time; they become mushy and the starch clouds the soup.

cumin-carrot soup with israeli couscous

Status: Meat or Dairy

Prep Time: 10 minutes

Cook Time: 30 minutes

Yield: 6–8 servings

fine sea salt

1 cup raw Israeli couscous

1 tablespoon olive oil

1 onion, cut into ¼-inch dice

2 stalks celery, cut into ¼-inch dice

1 teaspoon ground cumin, plus more for garnish

⅛ teaspoon ground turmeric

⅛ teaspoon ground nutmeg

1 pound carrots, peeled and sliced into thin discs, or 1-pound bag of pre-sliced carrots

6 cups chicken or vegetable stock

1½ cups soy milk or light cream

freshly ground black pepper

sour cream or nondairy sour cream, such as Tofutti brand, for garnish

fresh chives or parsley, finely chopped, for garnish

In a medium pot, bring 1¼ cups water and ½ teaspoon salt to a boil. Add the couscous and cover. Remove from heat. Set aside.

Heat the olive oil in a large pot over medium heat. Add the onion and celery. Sauté until translucent, 5–6 minutes. If the onions start to brown, lower the heat.

Meanwhile, in a small bowl or measuring cup, mix the cumin, turmeric, and nutmeg. Swirl or stir to combine. Add the spice mixture to the onions. Toast the spices for 2 minutes, until fragrant. Add the carrots and cook, stirring occasionally, for 3 minutes.

Add the stock and simmer, uncovered, for 15–20 minutes, until the carrots are soft.

Turn the heat off. With an immersion blender right in the pot, purée the soup until smooth and creamy. This can also be done in a blender or food processor fitted with a metal blade. Add the soy milk or cream and 1 teaspoon salt.

Taste the soup and season with more salt, if necessary, and pepper.

Place a mound of the couscous in the center of each shallow bowl.

Ladle the soup around the couscous.

As an optional garnish, you can add a dollop of sour cream. Add a light circular sprinkle of cumin and top with some chopped chives.

This soup can be made in advance but prepare and add the couscous right before serving. Israeli couscous is a pasta. It is a larger version of more traditional couscous, sometimes called pearl couscous. It will become overcooked and sticky if left in the soup.

hot and sour soup

Status: Meat

Prep Time: 10 minutes

Cook Time: 15 minutes

Yield: 6 servings

2 tablespoons canola oil

4 ounces shiitake mushroom caps, sliced

½ teaspoon ground ginger

3½ ounces oyster mushrooms, sliced

⅓ cup bamboo shoots, thinly sliced into matchsticks, or pre-sliced bamboo shoot strips

2 tablespoons soy sauce

5 tablespoons rice vinegar, divided

1 tablespoon honey

1 teaspoon Worcestershire sauce (see note on facing page)

5 cups chicken stock

¼ teaspoon freshly ground black pepper

⅛ teaspoon crushed red pepper flakes

⅛ teaspoon ground white pepper

2 teaspoons roasted or toasted sesame oil

1 tablespoon cornstarch, dissolved in 3 tablespoons water

5-6 Napa cabbage leaves, shredded

4 scallions, thinly sliced, white and pale green parts only

1 large egg white, slightly beaten with a fork

Heat the oil in a large pot over medium heat. Add the shiitake mushroom caps and the ginger. Sauté for 2 minutes. Add the oyster mushrooms and bamboo shoots. Cook for 1 minute. The mushrooms should start to soften.

Add the soy sauce, 2 tablespoons rice vinegar, honey, Worcestershire sauce, stock, black pepper, red pepper flakes, and white pepper. Bring to a boil.

Mix in the sesame oil and the dissolved cornstarch. Add the shredded cabbage and the scallions. Bring to a simmer.

Slowly pour the egg white into the soup in a steady stream and with a fork stir in one direction only, stirring slowly for thick strands of egg, more rapidly for thinner strands. Remove from heat and immediately stir in the remaining 3 tablespoons of rice vinegar.

Ladle into bowls.

If there was ever a Chinese Take-Out Hall-of Fame, hot-and-sour soup would top the list. This streamlined version will get it fresh, hot, and on the table in record time, without any sacrifice in taste or texture. For a heartier dish, you can add shredded chicken or small cubes of firm tofu that has been drained.

A note about Worcestershire sauce:

All Worcestershire sauce contains anchovies. If the kosher certification mark stands alone, then the percentage of anchovies is less than 1.6% of the whole product. Many rabbinical authorities say that this is okay to use with meat.

If the kosher certification on the label has a fish notation next to it, the level exceeds 1.6% and you should refrain from using it in meat dishes.

pumpkin bisque

Status: Meat or Parve

Prep Time: 5 minutes

Cook Time: 15 minutes

Yield: 8 servings

1 tablespoon olive oil

2 cloves fresh garlic, coarsely chopped

6 cups chicken or vegetable stock

2 (15-ounce) cans pure pumpkin, NOT pumpkin pie filling

¼ cup pure maple syrup

1 tablespoon sugar

fine sea salt

1 teaspoon dried ground sage

1 teaspoon ground cinnamon

½ teaspoon onion powder

raw pumpkin seeds, for garnish

In a large pot, heat the olive oil over medium heat. Add the garlic. Cook for 1 minute, stirring occasionally. Add the stock and pumpkin. Add the maple syrup, sugar, 1 teaspoon salt, sage, cinnamon, and onion powder. With an immersion blender or whisk, blend until very smooth.

Bring to a simmer. Cook for 10 minutes. Taste and season with more salt if necessary.

Ladle into bowls. Garnish with raw pumpkin seeds.

A bisque is a thick, rich soup that usually contains seafood. While this one does not, it is so thick and rich I thought it deserved to be called a bisque. More importantly, when you have little time to get a bowl of something warm and delicious on the table, this soup is your answer. I serve it with a loaf of crusty bread to sop up every last drop from the bowl.

Kosher by Design Short on Time

escarole eggdrop soup

Status: Meat or Parve

Prep Time: 5 minutes

Cook Time: 15 minutes

Yield: 6 servings

½ head escarole

1 tablespoon olive oil

5 scallions, sliced, white and pale green parts only

7 cups chicken or vegetable stock

½ teaspoon fine sea salt

¼ teaspoon freshly ground black pepper

1½ tablespoons cornstarch

2 eggs, beaten with a whisk

6 chives, finely chopped

12 fresh snow peas, sliced on the diagonal

Separate the escarole into individual leaves. Pile the leaves. Trim off the white root end. Dice the leaves. Set aside.

Heat the olive oil in a large pot over medium heat. Add the scallions and cook, stirring and shaking the pan for 2–3 minutes or until shiny; do not allow them to brown. Add half the stock. Let the stock come to a boil; season with salt and pepper.

In a separate bowl, stir the remaining stock and cornstarch until the cornstarch dissolves. Add this mixture to the pot. Return the soup to a simmer.

Slowly pour the beaten eggs into the soup in a steady stream and gently stir it with a fork in one direction only, stirring slowly for thick strands of egg, more rapidly for thinner strands.

Add the escarole and allow to wilt for 2 minutes.

Mix in the chives and snow peas. Simmer for 2 minutes.

Ladle into bowls.

My friend and teacher, Chef Damian Sansonetti from Shallots Restaurant and DB Bistro Moderne, taught me how to make this soup, which is based on Italian Wedding Soup, minus the meatballs. The chef has some Italian heritage and has enjoyed many a cup of this soup, although never at a wedding! To me it is closer to an egg-drop soup with the colorful and nutritious addition of the green escarole. Either way, it is hot, healthy and filling. Now that's something to hora about!

Kosher by Design Short on Time

tomato spinach rice soup

Status: Meat or Parve

Prep Time: 5 minutes

Cook Time: 30 minutes

Yield: 6–8 servings

2 tablespoons olive oil

1 medium onion, cut into ¼-inch dice

2 cloves fresh garlic, thinly sliced

12 ounces tomato juice

1 (28-ounce) can diced tomatoes, liquid reserved

4 cups chicken or vegetable stock

⅓ cup raw sushi rice

1 teaspoon fresh chopped dill

6 fresh chives, thinly sliced

¾ cup fresh baby spinach leaves, stacked and thinly sliced

½ teaspoon dried basil

½ teaspoon dried oregano

fine sea salt

freshly ground black pepper

Heat the oil in a large pot over medium heat. Add the onion and garlic and cook for 3–4 minutes until shiny and translucent; if the onions start to brown, lower the heat.

Add the tomato juice, diced tomatoes, stock, and rice. Stir in the dill, chives, sliced spinach leaves, basil, and oregano.

Cover the pot and simmer for 20 minutes over medium-low heat.

Season with salt and pepper.

Ladle into bowls.

The sushi rice is a nice touch as it is thicker and starchier than long-grain rice and adds great texture. Look for it in the Asian section of the supermarket. As with any soup that includes rice of any kind, it is best served right off the stove. When the soup sits overnight, the rice absorbs the liquid and turns mushy.

SALADS

sautéed vegetable and lentil salad

Status: Parve

Prep Time: 15 minutes

Cook Time: 10 minutes

Yield: 8–10 servings

1 Asian eggplant, unpeeled or small Italian eggplant, peeled, cut into ¾-inch dice

1 medium yellow squash, with skin, cut into ½-inch dice

1 medium zucchini, with skin, cut into ½-inch dice

3 portobello mushroom caps, cut into ½-inch dice

½ red onion, cut into ¼-inch dice

1 red bell pepper, seeded and cut into ¼-inch dice

¼ cup balsamic vinegar

½ cup plus 1 tablespoon extra-virgin olive oil, divided

1 (1-ounce) packet Good Seasons Italian Dressing mix

1 (15-ounce) can lentils, drained and rinsed

1 (15-ounce) can chickpeas (garbanzo beans), drained and rinsed

fine sea salt

freshly ground black pepper

Place all the diced vegetables into a large bowl.

Pour the balsamic vinegar, ½ cup olive oil, and seasoning packet into a cruet or jar and shake or whisk to combine. Pour over the vegetables.

Heat 1 tablespoon olive oil in large skillet over medium heat.

Add the vegetables and their dressing. Sauté until shiny and softened, 5–6 minutes. Remove from heat. Transfer to a bowl.

Add the lentils and chickpeas. Mix to combine. Season with salt and pepper.

Serve warm or at room temperature.

This salad is a kaleidoscope of color. It is great at a barbecue or as a side to a simple chicken dish. Plus, the canned lentils and chickpeas and the packaged salad dressing mix make this truly fast and easy.

warm mushroom-potato salad

Status: Parve
Prep Time: 5 minutes
Cook Time: 25 minutes
Yield: 6–8 servings

2 pounds baby red potatoes, halved

2 tablespoons olive oil

6 ounces shiitake mushrooms caps, cut into ½-inch dice

3 scallions, thinly sliced, white and pale green parts only

1 shallot, thinly sliced

⅛ teaspoon dried thyme

⅛ teaspoon dried sage

⅛ teaspoon ground marjoram

⅛ teaspoon dried basil

2 cloves fresh garlic, minced

2 tablespoons soy sauce

1 teaspoon fine sea salt

1 teaspoon freshly ground black pepper

⅓ cup mayonnaise

2 tablespoons apple-cider vinegar

¼ cup chopped fresh parsley leaves

Place the potatoes into a medium pot. Cover with water. Bring to a boil over medium heat and cook for about 20 minutes or until the potatoes are tender when pierced with a fork. Drain and return to the pot.

Meanwhile, heat the oil in a medium skillet over medium heat. Add the mushrooms, scallions, shallot, thyme, sage, marjoram, and basil. Sauté for 4–5 minutes, until the shallots and mushrooms are softened.

Add the mushroom mixture to the drained potatoes.

In a small bowl mix the minced garlic, soy sauce, salt, pepper, mayonnaise, vinegar, and parsley. Add to the pot and toss to coat the potatoes.

Serve warm or at room temperature.

Certain foods remind us of certain people. Potato salads will always be a small reminder of my friend Lisa Goldenberg Altman, an extraordinary woman, who passed away at far too early an age. In addition to being a wonderful wife, mother, and lawyer, she was passionate about many things, including cooking. She had created dozens of versions of potato salad, which were in her recipe box. This one is a winning combination of some of those.

balsamic chicken panzanella

Status: Meat

Prep Time: 10 minutes

Cook Time: 20 minutes

Yield: 6 servings

1 (12-inch) French baguette or Italian bread

2 tablespoons balsamic vinegar, divided

5 tablespoons olive oil, divided

1 teaspoon dried rosemary, divided

2 boneless, skinless chicken breast halves

fine sea salt

freshly ground black pepper

1 small (or ½ medium) red onion, thinly sliced

2 medium tomatoes, cored and cut into 1-inch chunks

½ cup fresh mint leaves, coarsely chopped

⅓ cup extra-virgin olive oil, plus more for garnish

Preheat oven to 350°F. Line a cookie sheet with parchment paper. Set aside.

Slice the bread into 1-inch slices; cut each slice into 1-inch cubes. Place into a bowl. Drizzle with 1 tablespoon balsamic vinegar and 3 tablespoons olive oil. Crumble half the rosemary over the bread. Toss. Not every piece will be completely coated. Arrange in a single layer on the prepared cookie sheet. Bake for 12 minutes, until toasted but not dried out. The centers should still be somewhat soft.

Meanwhile, season the chicken with salt and pepper on each side. Slice each lengthwise into 3 strips and then crosswise to make 1-inch cubes similar in size to the bread cubes.

Over medium-high, heat 1–2 tablespoons olive oil in a skillet large enough to hold the chicken cubes without crowding; you should still be able to see some pan between the cubes. Crumble in the remaining rosemary. When the oil is hot, add the chicken and sauté for 2–3 minutes. Turn each piece and cook for an additional 2–3 minutes. Set aside.

Place the red onions, tomatoes, and mint into a large bowl. Pour the ⅓ cup extra-virgin olive oil and remaining tablespoon of balsamic vinegar over the salad. Add the chicken cubes. Toss to coat. Add the toasted bread cubes. Toss again. Season with salt and pepper.

Divide onto individual plates. Add a drizzle of extra-virgin olive oil around each plate if desired.

Panzanella is an Italian-style bread salad that is as colorful as it is intensely flavored. You can make this a dairy salad by substituting chunks or balls of hand-rolled mozzarella for the chicken. It works wonderfully on a brunch table with this cheese option.

The baguette or Italian bread works best, but in a pinch, you can use bagels. You need a bread that will show some resistance and not become soaked or too mushy from the balsamic and oil.

Make the components of this recipe ahead of time and toss it together right before serving.

edamame salad

Status: Parve

Prep Time: 5 minutes

Cook Time: none

Yield: 6 servings

5 leaves romaine lettuce

4 ounces mesclun or spring mix lettuces

1½ cups (8 ounces) shelled edamame

1 cup grape tomatoes, halved

¼ teaspoon fleur de sel or coarse sea salt

⅓ cup extra-virgin olive oil

2 tablespoons balsamic vinegar

¾ teaspoon fresh thyme leaves

¼ teaspoon cayenne pepper

¼ teaspoon freshly ground black pepper

handful of soy nuts (also called roasted and salted soybeans)

Stack the romaine leaves on a work surface. With a sharp knife, shred them and place into your salad bowl. Add the mesclun, edamame, and tomato halves. Sprinkle with the fleur de sel or coarse sea salt.

In a jar or container, whisk or shake the olive oil, balsamic vinegar, thyme, cayenne pepper, and black pepper.

Pour the dressing over the salad and toss to mix. Sprinkle in the soy nuts.

Transfer to chilled salad plates.

Edamame are fresh soybeans. They are delicious and healthy as they are high in protein, fiber, and isoflavones, which are said to prevent heart disease and cancer. Some supermarkets sell the shelled edamame fresh in the produce section, but you can also buy them frozen and cook them for 5 minutes in boiling salted water. Drain and then shock them in cold water to stop the cooking; then pat dry. If you can only find edamame in the shell, that's fine too; just remove them and discard the shell.

Soy nuts are whole soybeans that have been soaked in water and then baked until crisp. The salted ones are similar to peanuts and add great crunch to this salad.

cucumber dill salad

Status: Dairy or Parve

Prep Time: 5 minutes

Cook Time: none

Yield: 6–8 servings

3 English (hothouse) cucumbers, peeled

¾ cup sour cream or nondairy sour cream, such as Tofutti brand

1½ teaspoons fine sea salt

2 tablespoons chopped fresh dill

juice of ½ large lemon, or 1 tablespoon lemon juice

½ small red onion, very thinly sliced

Slice each cucumber in half lengthwise. With a melon baller or a spoon, scoop out and discard the seeds from each cucumber.

Cut each cucumber half into ¼-inch bias-cut slices. Place into a medium bowl.

Add the sour cream, salt, dill, lemon juice and red onion slices. Toss to combine.

Transfer to a chilled bowl or salad plates.

A classic — and no wonder! This recipe is quick, easy, cool, refreshing, and delicious. English (hothouse) cucumbers are usually sold wrapped in plastic at the supermarket. They are longer than other varieties and are said to be seedless, although I always scoop out the seeds when I am using them in a recipe. For the most part, the skin is thin and not waxed, so it can be eaten.

blackened mixed-grill salad

Status: Meat

Prep Time: 10 minutes

Cook Time: 20 minutes

Yield: 6 servings

½ pound (2 portions) skirt steak

2 boneless, skinless chicken breast halves, tenders separated

blackening spice blend, such as the Paul Prudhumme Blackened Redfish Magic brand

1 tablespoon canola oil

½ cup grape tomatoes, halved

½ head romaine lettuce, thinly sliced into shreds

½ small red onion, halved and thinly sliced

DRESSING:

¼ cup mayonnaise

1 tablespoon plus 1 teaspoon lemon juice

½ teaspoon dried oregano

½ teaspoon hot sauce, such as Tabasco

¼ teaspoon garlic powder

fleur de sel or coarse sea salt

Season both sides of the steak, chicken breasts, and tenders with a light sprinkling of the blackening spice. Pat lightly to press the spices into the surface of the meat.

Heat the oil in a large skillet until very hot and almost smoking. Gently place the steak and chicken into the pan in a single layer and sear. Cook the steak for 4 minutes per side and the chicken for 7–8 minutes per side. Allow both the meat and chicken to rest for a few minutes on a platter or cutting board before slicing.

Immediately add the tomato halves to the pan so they can soak up the flavor from any juices and browned bits. Sauté for 1–2 minutes to soften slightly.

Place the romaine into a mixing bowl. Toss with the onion slices.

In a small bowl, mix the mayonnaise with the lemon juice, oregano, hot sauce, and garlic powder. Dress the lettuce and onions with half the dressing. Place on a platter or individual plates and top with the grilled tomatoes.

Thinly slice the meat and chicken on a diagonal. Fan the slices over the salad.

Drizzle with the remaining dressing. Sprinkle lightly with the fleur de sel or coarse sea salt.

Kosher skirt steak is a very salty cut of meat and has a distinctive flavor. If you like, you can soak the meat for a few hours to remove some of the saltiness, or use filet split or London broil in its place.

baby blue salad

Status: Dairy

Prep Time: 5 minutes

Cook Time: none

Yield: 6–8 servings

½ cup canola oil

¼ cup rice vinegar

1 pint fresh blueberries, divided

¼ teaspoon yellow mustard

2 tablespoons apple juice or water

6-7 ounces baby arugula

¼ cup sweetened dried cranberries, such as Craisins, or dried blueberries

1 handful shelled walnuts, chopped

8 ounces blue cheese crumbles

Place the oil into a quart-sized or other tall container. Add the vinegar, ½ cup blueberries, mustard, and apple juice or water. With an immersion blender, process until thoroughly combined. Set aside.

Place the arugula into a large salad bowl. Stir the dressing with a spoon if it has thickened. Lightly dress the arugula with the blueberry dressing to taste. Sprinkle on the remaining fresh blueberries, cranberries, and walnuts. Top with blue cheese.

Blueberries in both the dressing and the salad make this sweet-spicy dish a standout. And what a lovely way to make the most of summer's luscious blueberries!

apple walnut salad with creamy cider dressing

Status: Dairy or Parve

Prep Time: 10 minutes

Cook Time: none

Yield: 6 servings

2 Granny Smith apples, cored and thinly sliced

2 teaspoons lemon juice

fine sea salt

freshly ground black pepper

½ cup sour cream or nondairy sour cream, such as Tofutti brand

¼ cup apple cider

½ teaspoon sugar

⅛ teaspoon ground cinnamon

⅛ teaspoon ground nutmeg

½ cup walnut halves

1 head endive lettuce, separate

4 ounces mesclun lettuce or micro greens

sweetened dried cranberries, such as Craisins

Place the sliced apples into a bowl and toss with the lemon juice to hold the color. Season with salt and pepper.

In a small bowl, whisk the sour cream with the apple cider, sugar, cinnamon, and nutmeg. Set aside.

On 6 salad plates, arrange the apples in concentric circles of overlapping slices to form a "bed" on each plate.

Sprinkle walnuts over each plate.

Dip the endive leaves into the dressing, shaking off excess. Stack the leaves in a pile in the center of the apples, in a haphazard way, on each plate.

Lightly dress the mesclun leaves. Bunch a handful of mesclun on top of each endive pile. Sprinkle the cranberries over each plate for some color.

This salad lends itself to such beautiful presentation you'll want to make it time and again. I love what a wonderful sweet salad it is, yet there is almost no sugar in the dressing. The apple-pie spices trick your brain into thinking it is eating something sweet. You can used Emerald brand Glazed Toffee Walnuts in place of plain ones if you do want to add extra sweetness and crunch. If the season is right, replace the Craisins with fresh pomegranate seeds.

antipasto pasta salad

Status: Meat

Prep Time: 15 minutes

Cook Time: 10 minutes

Yield: 8–10 servings

8 ounces (½ box) rotini or bow-tie pasta, cooked al dente

3 leaves romaine lettuce, thinly sliced

1 roasted red pepper (if using from a jar, rinse well), cut into ¼-inch dice

½ small red onion, very thinly sliced

¾ cup canned sliced black olives

2 sun-dried tomatoes, packed in oil, coarsely chopped

1 (15-ounce) can chickpeas (garbanzo beans), drained and rinsed

1 shallot, minced

6 ounces (½ small) salami, cut into ¼-inch dice

¼ pound cooked Mexican-style turkey breast, such as the Hod brand, cut into ¼-inch dice (if you can't find the turkey, use an additional ¼ pound salami)

3 pepperoncini, drained and very thinly sliced

DRESSING:

½ cup red-wine vinegar

1 tablespoon balsamic vinegar

¼ teaspoon dried oregano

¼ teaspoon dried thyme

¼ teaspoon dried basil

¼ teaspoon fine sea salt

¼ teaspoon freshly ground black pepper

⅓ cup extra-virgin olive oil

leaves of 3 sprigs flat Italian parsley, coarsely chopped, for garnish

In a large bowl, combine the sliced romaine lettuce, roasted red pepper, red onion, olives, sun-dried tomatoes, chickpeas, shallot, salami, turkey, and pepperoncini.

Toss together with the pasta.

Pour the vinegars over the salad. Sprinkle in the oregano, thyme, basil, salt, and pepper. Drizzle with the olive oil.

Toss to completely combine and coat the vegetables and pasta. Transfer to serving bowl or individual dishes.

Sprinkle on the parsley leaves.

This salad gets better with age, so feel free to make it a day or two in advance. It also travels well, which makes it a good choice to take to a party or picnic.

asian barbecue salmon salad

Status: Parve

Prep Time: 10 minutes

Cook Time: 15 minutes

Yield: 6 servings

1¼ pounds fresh salmon fillet, skin and all pinbones removed

½ cup favorite barbecue sauce

2 teaspoons teriyaki sauce

3 teaspoons roasted or toasted sesame oil, divided

½ teaspoon garlic powder

¼ teaspoon wasabi powder

1 large head romaine lettuce, coarsely chopped

½ English (hothouse) cucumber, unpeeled, sliced into ¼-inch half-moons

fine sea salt

freshly ground black pepper

2 tablespoons fresh lemon juice

black and white sesame seeds, for garnish

Preheat oven to 350°F. Spray a baking pan or broiler pan with nonstick cooking spray. Set aside.

Cut the salmon into 2-inch cubes. Set aside.

In a medium bowl, whisk the barbecue sauce, teriyaki sauce, and 2 teaspoons sesame oil, garlic powder, and wasabi powder.

Add the salmon cubes to the bowl and toss to coat.

Place the salmon in a single layer into the prepared pan and bake for 10–12 minutes or until cooked through.

In a bowl, combine the lettuce and sliced cucumbers. Season with salt and pepper. Toss with lemon juice and 1 teaspoon sesame oil.

Place the salmon cubes on top of the salad. Garnish with black and white sesame seeds.

Salmon is a great source of the omega-3 fatty acids, a type of fat that provides a wide array of health benefits. Atlantic salmon is generally farmed and Pacific is generally wild. There is a difference in taste, color, and price between the two, just as there is debate as to which is healthier. Vary the type of salmon you buy and see which you like better.

citrusy chicken salad with warm olive vinaigrette

Status: Meat

Prep Time: 10 minutes

Cook Time: 15 minutes

Yield: 6 servings

4 boneless, skinless chicken breast halves, pounded slightly

fine sea salt

freshly ground black pepper

3 tablespoons olive oil, divided

1 head romaine lettuce, chopped into bite-sized pieces

juice of 1 lemon

1 (11-ounce) can mandarin oranges, juice reserved

1½ teaspoons lime juice

12 pimiento-stuffed green Spanish olives, drained and quartered

12 pitted black olives, drained and quartered

1 ruby-red grapefruit, peeled and segmented

2 limes, peeled and segmented

1 cup red grape tomatoes, halved

Season the chicken breasts with salt and pepper.

Heat 2 tablespoons olive oil in a medium skillet over medium heat. Add the chicken and sear for 5–6 minutes. Turn the chicken over and cook on the other side for 5–6 minutes or until cooked through and no longer pink. Remove from the pan.

Meanwhile, place the romaine on a platter or in salad bowl.

In a small bowl, whisk the lemon juice, juice from the can of mandarin oranges, and the lime juice.

With the skillet still on the stove and the heat at medium, add 2 tablespoons of the citrus juice, the remaining tablespoon of olive oil, and olives to the pan. Sauté until just heated through, about 45 seconds. Toss the olives with any pan juices into the greens.

Slice the chicken on the diagonal into thin slices. Add to the salad.

Add the mandarin oranges, grapefruit segments, lime segments, and tomatoes. Toss with any remaining citrus juices. Serve warm or at room temperature.

Whether it is a lime, lemon, grapefruit, or orange, for pristine citrus segments follow these directions: Cut a slice off the top and bottom of the fruit to expose the flesh and allow it to stand flat. Using a paring knife, cut the skin and white pith, following the round contoured shape of the fruit and being careful not to cut too much of the flesh. Trim off any remaining pith. Hold the fruit over a bowl to catch any juices. With the paring knife, cut on either side of each membrane to release a citrus segment. Let them fall into the bowl as you make your way around the fruit. You can squeeze what is left of the fruit for the juice.

grilled beef and radish salad

Status: Meat

Prep Time: 5 minutes

Cook Time: 10 minutes

Yield: 6 servings

1½ pounds London broil or filet split

fine sea salt

freshly ground black pepper

2 tablespoons olive oil

1 daikon radish (look for a small one, about the size of a parsnip), peeled

3 red radishes, thinly sliced

2 cups sprouts, any kind

1 cup baby arugula

½ cup chopped fresh parsley

¼ cup chopped fresh cilantro

¼ cup extra-virgin olive oil

2 tablespoons lime juice

Thinly slice the steak on the bias. Season the slices with salt and pepper.

Heat the 2 tablespoons olive oil in a large skillet over medium heat. Add the meat and sear for 2–3 minutes per side, using tongs to turn the pieces. Remove the steak slices as they are done and set the meat aside.

Cut the daikon in half lengthwise. Thinly slice into half-moons.

Place the daikon and red radish into a large mixing bowl. Add the sprouts and arugula.

Add the parsley and cilantro. Toss in ¼ cup of extra-virgin olive oil and lime juice.

Arrange the salad on a plate or platter and lay the beef slices on top.

Serve warm or at room temperature.

Radish is a root vegetable. Both the bulb and the leaves are edible, though I call just for the bulbs in this recipe. The leaves tend to be on the bitter side. Daikon radish is shaped like a large carrot but is white in color. It can be eaten raw, although it is often used in Japanese stir-fry dishes. I love its crunch in this salad. Be sure to wash it well and peel just a thin layer from the outside.

spinach strawberry banana salad

Status: Parve
Prep Time: 10 minutes
Cook Time: none
Yield: 6–8 servings

¾ cup vegetable or canola oil
¾ cup sugar
½ cup white vinegar
1 teaspoon dried minced onion
½ teaspoon dry mustard powder
½ teaspoon Worcestershire sauce
½ teaspoon paprika
2 teaspoons poppy seeds

2 teaspoons toasted sesame seeds
3 bananas, peeled, cut into ¼-inch slices
lemon juice
6 ounces fresh baby spinach leaves
3 cups strawberries (1 quart), stems removed, cut into ¼-inch slices
½ cup chopped walnuts

In a blender or food processor fitted with a metal blade, or with an immersion blender, combine the oil, sugar, vinegar, minced onion, mustard powder, Worcestershire sauce, and paprika. Blend or pulse until emulsified. Add the poppy seeds and sesame seeds. Shake or stir to combine.

Place the banana slices in a small bowl and sprinkle with lemon juice to hold the color.

Place half the spinach leaves into a glass bowl. Layer with half the strawberries and half the bananas. Drizzle with some of the dressing. Sprinkle on half the walnuts. Repeat with the remaining spinach, strawberries, bananas, dressing, and walnuts.

Janet Pernick, one of my Mom's oldest friends, called me one day to tell me that she was planning just the type of dinner party that I love. She had a great but concise menu filled with interesting recipes, a fun tablescape planned, and an eclectic group of people on the guest list. Because many of the recipes were from my books, she had a few questions. After chatting for over an hour she said, "Okay, as payment for all the help, here's a treasure from my mah-jongg group," and with that she rattled off this recipe, which has since wowed my own mah-jongg group on more than one occasion!

heirloom tomato caprese salad

Status: Dairy

Prep Time: 10 minutes

Cook Time: none

Yield: 6 servings

6 heirloom tomatoes in a variety of shapes and colors

¾ teaspoon fine sea salt

¼ teaspoon freshly ground black pepper

16 basil leaves, purple if possible, gently torn by hand

3 ounces baby arugula

½ cup sliced roasted red peppers, jarred (if jar has pepper halves, use 2 halves, thinly sliced)

12 ounces fresh, hand-rolled mozzarella cheese

½ cup extra-virgin olive oil

¼ cup balsamic vinegar

Halve each tomato. Slice half the tomatoes into ¼-inch slices and cut the others into chunks. Place into a medium bowl. Sprinkle on salt and pepper. Toss. Add the torn basil leaves, arugula, and roasted red peppers. Toss to combine. Set aside.

Slice the cheese into ¼-inch slices. Set aside.

In a small bowl, stir the oil and balsamic vinegar. They will not emulsify; the separation is part of the beauty of this dressing. Spoon 2 tablespoons of the dressing onto the salad, tossing to coat. Make sure both oil and vinegar are in the spoon.

Pile a handful of the salad on each chilled salad plate. Arrange the cheese on the plates.

Drizzle more of the dressing around the plate, so that it pools around the perimeter of the salad.

Danger! Do not attempt this salad during the winter. It is a walk down the aisles of a farmer's market and it screams of summer. In my local farmer's market (the parking lot of the Walgreen's drug store), I have found the most incredible varieties of heirloom tomatoes. The colors and shapes are fabulous and the taste is like no supermarket tomato I have ever tried. At markets like this, or at specialty stores, you can sometimes find purple basil, which is a nice touch to this already colorful salad as well.

Tomatoes love salt and it really brightens their flavor, so don't leave it out. Feel free to add extra after the salad is dressed.

thai chicken coconut rice salad

Status: Meat

Prep Time: 15 minutes

Cook Time: 25 minutes

Yield: 6 servings

1½ cups raw sushi rice, rinsed until water runs clear, and drained

2½ cups water

¾ cup coconut milk (NOT cream of coconut)

2 tablespoons sugar

fine sea salt

1 tablespoon canola oil

3 tablespoons lime juice, divided

4 boneless, skinless chicken breast halves, tenders separated

1 green bell pepper, seeded and very thinly sliced into 2-inch strips

1 small red onion, very thinly sliced

1 jalapeño or serrano chili, seeds and ribs removed, finely minced

¼ cup fresh basil leaves, shredded

½ cup fresh mint leaves, shredded

THAI DRESSING:

½ cup lime juice

3 tablespoons teriyaki sauce

2 tablespoons coconut milk

1 tablespoon sugar

pinch of freshly ground black pepper

pinch of ground ginger

1 clove fresh garlic, minced

3 fresh basil leaves

7 fresh mint leaves

½ cup canola oil

Place the drained rice, water, coconut milk, sugar, and ¼ teaspoon salt into a medium pot. Stir once. Bring to a simmer over medium-low heat. Simmer for 5–10 minutes. Cover the pot and let it stand off the heat for 20–25 minutes. Fluff before serving.

Meanwhile, heat the canola oil in a large skillet over medium heat. Season the chicken with salt and pepper and drizzle with 1 tablespoon of lime juice. Add the chicken breasts and tenders to the skillet. Sear for 5–6 minutes. Turn and cook for 5–6 minutes, until cooked through. Let the chicken stand for 5 minutes. Thinly slice on the diagonal. Place into a mixing bowl.

Toss the chicken slices with the green bell pepper, red onion, jalapeño or serrano chili, basil leaves, and mint leaves. Sprinkle in ½ teaspoon salt.

Prepare the dressing: Combine the lime juice, teriyaki sauce, coconut milk, sugar, pepper, ginger, ⅛ teaspoon salt, garlic, basil, and mint in a tall quart-sized container. Purée with an immersion blender. Drizzle in the oil and blend to create an emulsion and mixture is slightly thickened.

Toss the rice and chicken with the Thai dressing.

seared ahi tuna nicoise

Status: Parve

Prep Time: 15 minutes

Cook Time: 5 minutes

Yield: 6 servings

3 (8-ounce) ahi tuna steaks

fine sea salt

freshly ground black pepper

1 tablespoon olive oil, divided

6 ounces baby arugula or spring mix

3 tablespoons extra-virgin olive oil, plus more for drizzling

1 tablespoon lemon juice

1 small bulb fennel, fronds and ½-inch of base trimmed and discarded, bulb halved and very thinly sliced

1½ cups grape tomatoes, halved

1 (7-ounce) jar Nicoise, Kalamata, or Gaeta olives, pitted and coarsely chopped

6 scallions, thinly sliced on the diagonal

3 hard-boiled eggs, peeled and sliced lengthwise into quarters

fleur de sel or coarse sea salt

6 giant bread croutons, optional (see note on facing page)

Heat an empty grill pan or skillet over medium heat. Sprinkle both sides of each tuna steak with salt and pepper. Rub 1 teaspoon oil into each steak, spreading it evenly on both sides.

When the pan is hot, place the tuna into it and sear for 2–3 minutes per side; the tuna should still be pink inside. Do not overcook.

Place the arugula or spring mix into a medium bowl. Add 3 tablespoons extra-virgin olive oil, lemon juice, 1 teaspoon salt, and ½ teaspoon pepper. Toss to coat.

Place the lettuce onto 6 plates. Add fennel slices and tomato halves. Sprinkle with chopped olives and scallions.

Slice the tuna into ¼-inch slices and arrange on the salads. Lightly drizzle the tuna with additional olive oil and sprinkle with fleur de sel or coarse sea salt.

Arrange the quartered eggs on the plates. If desired, place a giant crouton on the side of each plate.

I love to serve this main-dish salad with a giant crouton to soak up the juices. Cut a loaf of Italian bread on the diagonal into thick slices. Rub a cut clove of fresh garlic over the crusts. Place on a parchment-lined cookie sheet. Drizzle with olive oil and bake at 400°F for 7–8 minutes until toasted. Serve each salad with a giant crouton. Everyone will love this!

To properly make hard-boiled eggs, place them in a small pot. Cover them with cold water and bring to a boil over medium heat. When the water boils, cover the pot, turn off the heat and allow the eggs to sit for 15 minutes.

cashew-spinach coleslaw

Status: Parve

Prep Time: 5 minutes

Cook Time: none

Yield: 8–10 servings

1 (16-ounce) bag coleslaw mix

3 ounces baby spinach leaves

¼ cup sugar

½ teaspoon ground ginger

¼ teaspoon fine sea salt

¼ teaspoon freshly ground black pepper

½ cup rice vinegar

¼ cup roasted or toasted sesame oil

3 tablespoons soy sauce

2 tablespoons red-wine vinegar

¾ cup roasted, salted cashews

¼ cup shelled raw sunflower seeds (not roasted or salted)

Empty the package of coleslaw mix into a large mixing bowl or Ziploc bag.

Roll a handful of the spinach into a tight mound on a work surface. Using a sharp knife, shred the spinach and add it to the coleslaw mix. Repeat until all the spinach is shredded.

In a cruet or jar, mix the sugar, ginger, salt, pepper, rice vinegar, sesame oil, soy sauce, and red-wine vinegar. Cover and shake to emulsify the dressing. Pour the dressing over the salad and allow the flavors to mingle and mellow for at least an hour. This can even be made a day in advance.

Just before serving, add the cashews and sunflower seeds and toss to combine.

This salad is very light, not to mention a snap to prepare. It goes great at a barbecue or with a simple roast chicken or steak. It's a terrific do-ahead-dish; just don't add the cashews and sunflower seeds until you are ready to serve.

POULTRY

kishka-stuffed chicken

Status: Meat

Prep Time: 10 minutes

Cook Time: 30 minutes

Yield: 6 servings

6 boneless, skinless chicken breast halves

1 kishka, defrosted, all casings removed

⅓ cup apricot preserves

1 cup corn flake crumbs

honey

Preheat oven to 350°F.

Place each chicken breast between 2 sheets of waxed paper or parchment paper. Using a rolling pin or meat pounder, pound to an even ¼-inch thickness.

Cut a 1-inch slice of kishka. Roll it into a log and place into the center of a flattened cutlet. Repeat with the remaining 5 chicken breasts. You may have leftover kishka. Roll the cutlets around the kishka, tucking in the ends.

Pour the corn flake crumbs into a plate or bowl.

Brush each chicken roll with apricot preserves and dip into corn flake crumbs, coating all sides. Place the chicken rolls, seam-side-down, into a baking pan.

Lightly drizzle each roll with honey.

Bake, uncovered, for 30 minutes. Allow to stand for 10 minutes. Lightly drizzle with more honey. Serve whole or sliced.

When I was growing up my family went out to the deli for dinner on many Sundays. One of the delicacies we would order was kishka, which came smothered in gravy. I still use kishka in my cholent, so there is always one hanging out in my freezer. It is a wonderful creamy filling in this chicken dish. The bright orange color is eye-catching.

orange chicken

Status: Meat

Prep Time: 10 minutes

Cook Time: 1 hr. 20 min.

Yield: 6–8 servings

2 chickens, cut into quarters

¾ cup dark-brown sugar

2 tablespoons dry mustard powder

¼ teaspoon ground nutmeg

2 tablespoons cornstarch

1 cup orange juice (not from concentrate)

1 (12-ounce) jar orange marmalade

2 navel oranges, very thinly sliced

Preheat oven to 375°F. Place the chicken pieces in single layers, skin-side-up, into two 9- by 13-inch baking pans.

In a medium bowl, with a fork, mix the brown sugar, mustard powder, nutmeg, and cornstarch. Stir in the orange juice. Pour half of the mixture over each pan of chicken.

With the back of a spoon, spread the top of each chicken piece with the marmalade.

Scatter paper-thin slices of orange over the chicken, leaving some skin exposed.

Bake, uncovered, for 1 hour. Baste with the pan juices and bake for an additional 15–20 minutes or until the oranges are a deep amber color and the chicken is fully cooked and no longer pink, or a meat thermometer inserted into the thickest part of the thigh reads 180°F.

Transfer to a bowl or platter.

This is an old family recipe from my Aunt Temmie, a real New England lady who is great in the kitchen. She raised her four children in Tivertown, a small town in Rhode Island, where the entire population is well under 10,000! It was hard to keep kosher there and she had to drive to Boston and Providence for kosher butchers. Once there, she stocked up on chicken and meat so that she could prepare favorite family dishes like this one.

If your pans don't fit into your oven side by side, you may need to bake the lower pan for an extra few minutes so that the orange slices will caramelize.

turkey marsala with artichokes

Status: Meat

Prep Time: 10 minutes

Cook Time: 15 minutes

Yield: 6 servings

6 white-meat turkey cutlets

fine sea salt

freshly ground black pepper

all-purpose flour

8 ounces crimini mushrooms, sliced

⅓ cup olive oil, divided

3 shallots, thinly sliced

2 (13.75-ounce) cans artichoke hearts or bottoms (not in oil), rinsed

1½ cups Marsala wine or sweet vermouth

1½ tablespoons nondairy sour cream, such as Tofutti brand

1½ tablespoons margarine, cut into 4 pieces

Season both sides of each turkey cutlet with salt and pepper. Lightly dust each cutlet with flour, shaking off the excess.

Toss the mushrooms with 3 tablespoons flour. Set aside.

Heat 3–4 tablespoons olive oil in a large skillet over medium heat. Add the turkey cutlets in a single layer, working in batches if necessary, and sear for 3 minutes. Flip the cutlets over and cook for about 3 minutes on the other side, removing them to a platter as they are done. Once all the cutlets are seared, heat 1–2 tablespoons olive oil in the pan and add the floured mushrooms and the shallots. Sauté for 4 minutes. Add the artichokes and heat through.

Turn off the heat and add the wine. Return to low heat and swirl and stir in the nondairy sour cream and margarine. Whisk as the margarine melts, until smooth.

Pour the mushroom and artichoke mixture over the turkey cutlets. Serve hot.

While trying to get my family into healthier eating habits, I discovered turkey cutlets. My butcher sells them like chicken cutlets. They cook very quickly so I can get a great dinner on the table in under 15 minutes.

lemon-pepper fried chicken

Status: Meat

Prep Time: 10 minutes

Cook Time: 10 minutes

Yield: 6 servings

4 boneless, skinless chicken breast halves

canola or vegetable oil

1½ cups all-purpose flour

1 tablespoon coarse black pepper or 2 teaspoons finely ground black pepper

zest and juice of 1 lemon

1½ cups cold water

4-5 ice-cubes

fine sea salt

1 cup mayonnaise

1 tablespoon chopped fresh dill or 1 teaspoon dried dill

Thinly slice the chicken into long, very thin, bias-cut strips. Set aside.

Pour oil into a heavy medium pot to come three-fourths of the way up the sides. Heat over medium to 350°F.

While the oil is heating, prepare the batter: In a medium metal bowl, whisk the flour, black pepper, zest, lemon juice, and 1½ cups cold water.

Add the ice-cubes, as tempura batter fries up better when it is cold. Add the strips of chicken and coat them with the batter.

Add the coated chicken strips, a few at a time, and fry them, turning occasionally, until golden-brown. Remove with a slotted spoon and drain on paper towels. Sprinkle with salt.

In a small bowl or container, mix the mayonnaise with the chopped dill, stirring to combine.

Serve the warm chicken strips with the dill mayonnaise.

A grown-up version of chicken fingers, this recipe will please eaters of all ages. The coating is a tempura batter that works well for zucchini, red bell pepper strips, and eggplant, as well.

fiesta turkey burgers

1 pound ground white-meat turkey

1 pound ground dark-meat turkey

1 tablespoon lime juice

1 teaspoon fine sea salt

½ teaspoon freshly ground black pepper

¼ teaspoon ground cumin

1 teaspoon dried oregano

1 teaspoon garlic powder

1 tablespoon canola oil

6 hamburger buns

1 red onion, very thinly sliced

1 ripe Haas avocado, peeled, pitted, and thinly sliced

store-bought salsa

In a medium mixing bowl, combine the white-meat turkey, dark-meat turkey, lime juice, salt, pepper, cumin, oregano, and garlic powder.

Divide the meat into 6 equal portions and form into patties. Set aside.

Pour the canola oil into a grill pan or medium skillet. Heat the pan over medium heat. Add burgers to pan. Cook 5 minutes per side. Try not to move the burgers around on the grill pan so you will get nice grill marks.

When you remove the turkey burgers from the pan, place the buns, cut-side down into the pan. This will toast them and at the same time they will pick up flavoring from the pan.

Assemble the burgers: Place a few slices of red onion on the bottom bun. Top with the turkey burger. Add a few slices of avocado to each burger.

Top with some salsa and the top of the bun.

My girlfriend Karen Finkelstein gave me a fabulous time-saving tip. When she brings home various meats from the butcher, she seasons them as per recipes she plans on using and then freezes them, labeled with the recipe title. This allows her to defrost meat that is ready to go into the oven. This recipe would be a perfect candidate for this time-saving technique. Season the mix of ground turkey, form the patties, and freeze. On a day when time is short, just pop them into the fridge in the morning and grill them right before dinner. Such a simple and smart idea!

primavera chicken

Status: Meat

Prep Time: 10 minutes

Cook Time: 2 hours

Yield: 6–8 servings

6-8 chicken legs, with bone and skin

6-8 chicken thighs, with bone and skin

1 yellow squash, unpeeled

1 green zucchini, unpeeled

1 quart cherry tomatoes, halved

1 (8-ounce) bottle Italian dressing, such as the Wish-Bone "Robusto" brand

Preheat oven to 350°F. Place the chicken pieces in single layers, skin-side-up, into two 9- by 13-inch baking pans.

Slice the squash and zucchini in half lengthwise and slice into 1-inch-thick half-moons. Scatter over the chicken. Toss on the halved tomatoes.

Shake the dressing and drizzle it over the chicken.

Bake, uncovered, for 2 hours.

Remove the chicken to a platter. Toss the vegetables in the pan liquid and then scatter them over the chicken.

Although "primavera" is the Italian word for "spring," I find that I turn to this recipe in the winter, when Shabbos comes early and I have no time at all to fuss. Tomatoes are not at their best in the winter, but the long roasting process of this recipe caramelizes them so that they taste sweet and delicious.

maple-walnut chicken with sweet potato aioli

Status: Meat

Prep Time: 10 minutes

Cook Time: 25 minutes

Yield: 6 servings

6 boneless, skinless chicken breast halves

½ cup chopped walnuts

¼ cup plus 2 tablespoons pure maple syrup (not pancake syrup), divided

fine sea salt

freshly ground black pepper

2 teaspoons canola oil

2 tablespoons Dijon mustard

¼ teaspoon dried thyme

1 cup panko bread crumbs

1½ cups canned sweet potatoes, drained

1½ tablespoons light-brown sugar

2 tablespoons mayonnaise

1½ tablespoons pure maple syrup, not pancake syrup

Preheat oven to 350°F. Line a baking pan with parchment paper. Set aside.

Place a chicken breast smooth-side-down on a cutting board. Lift up the tender and if necessary, make a cut to form a long pocket. Repeat with the remaining 5 chicken breasts.

Stuff each pocket with 1 tablespoon walnuts. Drizzle in 1 teaspoon maple syrup. Close up the pocket. Place pocket-side down on prepared pan. Repeat with remaining breasts. Sprinkle with salt and pepper. Combine the canola oil, Dijon mustard, and thyme. Brush each cutlet with this mixture.

Bake for about 18 minutes or until chicken is cooked through.

Meanwhile, in a small bowl, mix ¼ cup maple syrup and panko bread crumbs to make a paste.

After the cutlets are baked, remove from the oven and spoon and press on the panko paste to form a crust. Turn the oven to broil, return the chicken to the oven, and broil 6–8 inches from heat source for 2 minutes, until crust is golden-brown.

In a small pot, heat the sweet potatoes, smashing them with a fork or spoon. Mix in light-brown sugar. Turn off the heat and whisk in the mayonnaise and 1½ tablespoons maple syrup.

Serve each cutlet with a dollop of the aioli.

Panko bread crumbs are Japanese bread crumbs unlike any you have ever used. They are larger than regular bread crumbs and create a deliciously crisp and crunchy crust. They can be found in regular supermarkets in a white box under the Kikkoman brand. There are also specialty brands of panko that can be ordered over the Internet or found in kosher gourmet stores.

greek garlic chicken

Status: Meat
Prep Time: 5 minutes
Cook Time: 1 hour
Yield: 6–8 servings

2 chickens, cut into eighths
2 onions, cut into large chunks
2 lemons
12-16 sprigs fresh oregano
8 cloves fresh garlic, halved
fine sea salt
freshly ground black pepper

½ cup olive oil
1 cup white wine
1½ cups Kalamata olives, pitted and coarsely chopped
½ cup Kalamata olives, whole, for garnish

Preheat oven to 450°F. Place the chicken pieces in single layers, skin-side-up, into two 9- by 13-inch baking pans.

Add the onion chunks. Slice the lemons in half lengthwise. Squeeze the lemon halves over the chicken. Cut each lemon half into 4 pieces; add to the chicken.

Set aside 4 sprigs of oregano and strip the oregano leaves from the rest. Scatter the leaves and the stripped sprigs over the chicken; they will add their perfume to the dish.

Add the garlic and season with salt and pepper. Drizzle with the oil and wine. Toss the mixture together. Sprinkle the chopped olives over the chicken.

Bake, uncovered, for 45 minutes – 1 hour, or until chicken is fully cooked and no longer pink, or a meat thermometer inserted into the thickest part of the thigh reads 180°F.

Transfer to a platter and garnish with whole olives and reserved oregano sprigs.

Pitting Kalamata olives is a breeze. Just smack each olive with your palm and the pit pops right out. If you don't have Kalamata olives, you can use canned black olives, but the Kalamata are more authentic and richer-tasting.

I garnish this delicious dish with some of the ingredients used to flavor it, such as fresh oregano sprigs and whole olives. It brings some of those vibrant colors back to the dish.

kalmein

1 bag boil-in-bag white rice

2 tablespoons canola oil

2 (15-ounce) cans Oriental stir-fry vegetable mix, such as Season brand, drained

1 (15-ounce) can stir-fry baby corn, drained

1 (15-ounce) can straw mushrooms, drained

leftover roasted or rotisserie chicken, skin and bones discarded, meat torn

⅓ cup Dijon mustard mixed with ¼ cup water

¼ teaspoon ground white pepper

¼ teaspoon ground black pepper

¼ teaspoon fine sea salt

2 cups chow-mein noodles

In a small pot, prepare the bag of white rice according to package directions.

Meanwhile, heat the oil in a large skillet over medium heat. Add the vegetables, baby corn, and mushrooms. Heat through, 3–4 minutes. Add the torn chicken. Stir in the mustard/water mixture. Season with the white pepper, black pepper, and salt. Stir in the prepared rice.

Transfer to serving bowl and sprinkle with chow-mein noodles.

When their bachelor sons are leaving for law school, some mothers give advice on learning, some on dating, and some on keeping a clean apartment. My mother-in-law gave her son, my husband Kalman, her own special send-off: the cutest book of handwritten recipes. Each had a personalized title, like Lasagna Kalmania, Fruits Fishbein, and Eggplant Boats À La Captain Kal.

Here's one that has stayed with Kal all these years. It is a simple chow mein made hot and tasty with leftover Shabbos or rotisserie chicken.

mediterranean poached chicken

Status: Meat

Prep Time: 15 minutes

Cook Time: 30 minutes

Yield: 6 servings

6 boneless, skinless chicken breast halves, pounded very thin

fine sea salt

freshly ground black pepper

2 tablespoons olive oil

½ red onion, very finely diced

⅛ teaspoon ground turmeric

pinch of cayenne pepper

pinch of dried rosemary, crumbled

1 medium russet potato, peeled and cut into small cubes

1 red bell pepper, seeded and finely diced

1 green bell pepper, seeded and finely diced

1 rib celery, finely diced

2 cups chicken stock

½ cup Pinot Grigio or other white wine

zest and juice of 1 lemon

1 (15-ounce) can chickpeas (garbanzo beans), drained and rinsed

¼ cup pitted green Spanish olives, coarsely chopped

1 tablespoon olive oil, for garnish

1 lemon sliced into 6 slices, for garnish

Season the chicken with salt and pepper. Roll one chicken breast lengthwise into a long cylinder. Secure with 3 toothpicks and slice into thirds to yield 3 equal spirals. Keep the toothpicks in place. Repeat with the other 5 breasts.

Heat the oil in a large pot over medium heat. Add the red onion; sauté for 2 minutes. Add the turmeric, cayenne pepper, rosemary, and potato cubes. Sauté for 3–4 minutes, stirring with a wooden spoon. The starch from the potato will make it stick to the pot. Add the red bell pepper, green bell pepper, and celery. Pour in the stock and white wine. Add the juice and zest of the lemon. Bring to a simmer. Add the chickpeas and the secured chicken spirals. Cover and simmer for 10–15 minutes, or until the chicken is no longer pink.

Season with salt and pepper. Sprinkle in chopped olives.

To garnish this dish, heat 1 tablespoon of olive oil in a small skillet over medium heat. Add the lemon slices and sear until they start to brown.

Remove and discard the toothpicks. Serve 3 spirals with the vegetables and some of the broth. Garnish with a seared lemon slice.

This healthy winner is reminiscent of a stew, except it cooks very quickly. The gorgeous color comes from turmeric, which is the same spice that gives ballpark mustard its yellow color.

middle eastern couscous chicken

Status: Meat

Prep Time: 10 minutes

Cook Time: 15 minutes

Yield: 6 servings

4 dried dates

3 dried black Mission figs

2 cups chicken stock

zest and juice of 1 lemon

2 cups small-grained couscous

3 tablespoons olive oil

4 boneless, skinless chicken breast halves, cut into cubes

fine sea salt

freshly ground black pepper

1 red bell pepper, seeded and cut into ¼-inch dice

1 zucchini, unpeeled, thinly sliced into half-moons

2 cloves fresh garlic, minced

extra-virgin olive oil, for drizzling

Chop the dates and figs into small pieces. A food processor fitted with a metal blade does this quickly and easily, but you can use a sharp knife.

Bring the chicken stock, lemon zest, and the chopped dates and figs to a boil in a medium pot that has a lid. When the water just starts to boil, add the couscous. Cover the pot. Remove from the heat and set aside for 10 minutes.

Meanwhile, heat the olive oil in a medium or large skillet over medium heat. Season the chicken cubes with salt and pepper. Place the chicken into the hot pan and cook 2–3 minutes per side. Use tongs to turn the chicken.

Remove the chicken and add the red bell pepper, zucchini, and garlic to the same pan to pick up the flavor of the chicken. Cook the vegetables for 4–5 minutes or until softened.

Remove the lid from the couscous. Drizzle in 1 tablespoon extra-virgin olive oil and scrape with a fork in all directions to fluff the grains. Place the couscous on a platter; top with the vegetables and the chicken.

Drizzle with the lemon juice and more extra-virgin olive oil. Season to taste with more salt and pepper.

This is a healthful vibrant recipe, and an all-in-one dinner with the vegetables and side dish included. Once you start using couscous you will be hooked. It's ridiculously easy to prepare and everyone loves the rice-like pasta.

tomato basil chicken

Status: Meat

Prep Time: 10 minutes

Cook Time: 1½ hours.

Yield: 6–8 servings

2 chickens, cut into eighths

2 large beefsteak tomatoes, cut into large chunks

1 (8-ounce) bottle Italian dressing, such as the Wish-Bone "Robusto" brand

½ cup fresh basil leaves

4 cloves fresh garlic

5 sun-dried tomatoes, packed in oil

fresh basil leaves, for garnish

Preheat the oven to 350°F. Place the chicken pieces in single layers, skin-side-up, into two 9- by 13-inch baking pans. Set aside.

Place the chunks of tomatoes into a food processor fitted with a metal blade. Pulse to chop. Add the dressing, basil, garlic, and sun-dried tomatoes. Pulse to purée and emulsify.

Pour the tomato-basil dressing evenly over the chicken pieces.

Bake, uncovered, for 1 hour and 30 minutes or until chicken is fully cooked and no longer pink, or a meat thermometer inserted into the thickest part of the thigh reads 180°F.

Transfer to serving platter. Garnish with fresh basil leaves.

Besides tasting great, this chicken dish has a fabulous aroma. It will make your whole house smell amazing. The combination of the chopped tomatoes, garlic, and fresh basil give it some real eye-appeal, as well, which is sometimes hard to achieve with a chicken dish.

chicken and eggplant in garlic sauce

Status: Meat

Prep Time: 15 minutes

Cook Time: 20 minutes

Yield: 6 servings

canola or vegetable oil

1 cup plus 3 tablespoons cornstarch, divided

5 boneless, skinless chicken cutlets, very thinly sliced lengthwise

1 large purple eggplant, peeled or 2 Asian eggplants, with skin, sliced into 2-inch long by ½-inch wide sticks, like french fries

⅓ cup soy sauce

¼ cup hoisin sauce

¼ cup rice vinegar

6 cloves fresh garlic, minced

2 teaspoons hot sauce, such as Tabasco

Fill a large pot halfway with canola or vegetable oil. Heat the oil over medium heat to 350°F, using a thermometer to determine temperature. This can also be done in a deep-fryer.

Bring to a boil a second large pot filled halfway with water.

In a medium bowl, dissolve 1 cup cornstarch with 1 cup water. Add the sliced chicken to the mixture and toss to coat.

When the oil is hot, remove the chicken from the cornstarch mixture, shaking off the excess, and carefully drop a handful at a time into the hot oil. Fry for 2 minutes until opaque. Remove with a slotted spoon or small strainer and immediately lower into the pot of boiling water. After 30 seconds remove with a slotted spoon or strainer to a paper-towel-lined plate. Repeat with remaining chicken.

Mix the eggplant sticks into the remaining cornstarch mixture. Carefully lower them into the hot oil, fry, and then boil in the hot water. After all the eggplant is boiled, pour out the water.

In a small bowl, mix the 3 tablespoons cornstarch with the soy sauce, hoisin sauce, rice vinegar, minced garlic, and hot sauce. Set aside.

Return the chicken and eggplant to the empty water pot. Pour in the sauce mixture. Cook over medium heat, stirring constantly, until the sauce thickens and adheres to the chicken.

Every summer, my dad, Lenny Spector, sends me, my mom, and my sisters on a Spector Girls retreat at the Ocean Place Spa in Long Branch, NJ. We spend 3 glorious days together where we laugh from the minute the car pulls off until it drops us back at home. We relax, catch up, swim, walk, sing, are pampered, and, most importantly, we eat! There is an array of incredible kosher restaurants near the spa. We know the rules: new restaurants every year, no diet talk allowed, and everyone must order something different for sharing. The only exception is this dish from Chang Mao Sakura. It is so fabulous that it has been "grandfathered," like the restaurant itself and is allowed every year. The owner invited me into his kitchen to watch the dish being prepared. Here is a very close rendition for the home cook. Just thinking of it makes me dream about the Spa…only 187 days to go till the next retreat!

To simulate the authenticity of Chinese cooking, you will need to have 2 pots going, one of hot oil and one of hot water. This recipe is a bit more effort than the others in this book, but it is well worth it.

honey-nut-crusted turkey cutlets

Status: Meat

Prep Time: 5 minutes

Cook Time: 10 minutes

Yield: 6 servings

6 (6-ounce) turkey cutlets, pounded very thin

fine sea salt

freshly ground black pepper

2 (6-ounce) cans honey-roasted almonds, such as Blue Diamond brand

¼ cup teriyaki sauce, plus more for brushing

2 tablespoons red-currant jelly

Preheat the oven to 350°F. Line a cookie sheet with parchment paper.

Place the turkey cutlets on the prepared baking sheet. Season each with salt and pepper. Brush each cutlet with teriyaki sauce. Set aside.

In the bowl of a food processor fitted with a metal blade, process the nuts with 10 (2-second) pulses. Process for 10 seconds more if needed to finely chop the nuts without grinding them to a powder. Add the ¼ cup teriyaki sauce and the currant jelly. Pulse 2–3 times to form a sticky paste.

Spray a small offset metal spatula or the back of a spoon with nonstick cooking spray and use it to spread a thin, even layer of the nut mixture over the top of each turkey cutlet. Place into the oven and bake for 5–7 minutes or until cooked through.

Allow the cutlets to cool for a minute.

Serve whole or slice on the diagonal into ¾-inch slices. Fan out the slices.

Serve warm or at room temperature.

I love the touch of sweetness and the crunch that the honey-roasted almonds add to the turkey. It is a surprising but welcome flavor pairing that quickly dresses up ordinary turkey cutlets.

falafel-crusted chicken

Status: Meat

Prep Time: 15 minutes

Cook Time: 20 minutes

Yield: 6 servings

6 boneless, skinless chicken breast halves

3 cups falafel mix (about 15 ounces), weight will vary among brands, divided

olive oil

2 plum tomatoes

1 cucumber, peeled

prepared chummos

Slice each chicken breast in half horizontally and then into thin strips.

Set out 2 medium bowls. In the first bowl place 1 cup dry falafel mix. Place 2 cups of the mix into the second bowl.

Add 2½ cups of water to the second bowl and stir until fully combined. Allow the batter to rest for 10 minutes.

Meanwhile, pour olive oil into a large skillet to come three-fourths of the way up the sides and heat over medium.

Toss each chicken strip into the bowl of dry falafel mix, coating well. Shake off the excess.

Check the wet batter to make sure it is a spreadable, slightly liquid consistency. If it is too thick, mix in additional 1–2 tablespoons of water. Working quickly, dip the coated chicken strips into the batter and pat it on to form a crust. Add the chicken strips to the hot oil in the skillet in a single layer, leaving room between strips. Allow the crust to form before flipping to cook on the other side, about 4–5 minutes per side. Do this in batches as necessary. Discard any extra batter.

Meanwhile, cut the tomatoes and cucumbers into medium dice.

Serve the falafel chicken with the diced vegetables and a dollop of chummos.

When nothing will satisfy as much as a piece of moist chicken encrusted with a crunchy coating, try these. You can buy the falafel mix in any supermarket and then mix it with water to make a batter to coat the chicken. And that's the hard part! The chicken cooks in minutes for a quick meal.

chicken fajitas

Status: Meat

Prep Time: 10 minutes

Cook Time: 10 minutes

Yield: 6 servings

4 boneless, skinless chicken breast halves

2 tablespoons lime juice, plus extra for garnish

1 tablespoon garlic powder

2 teaspoons soy sauce

1 tablespoon dark-brown sugar

1 tablespoon taco or fajita seasoning (from a 1.25-ounce packet)

1 tablespoon olive oil

1 small onion, very thinly sliced

1 red bell pepper, seeded and cut into very thin strips

1 green bell pepper, seeded and cut into very thin strips

6 large flour tortillas

nondairy sour cream, such as the Tofutti brand

¼ cup fresh cilantro leaves, chopped

Cut the chicken breasts on the diagonal into thin strips. Place them into a medium bowl. Add the lime juice, garlic powder, soy sauce, brown sugar, and taco or fajita seasoning. Mix well.

Heat the olive oil in a large skillet over medium-high heat. Sauté the chicken in the skillet for 5 minutes or until cooked through.

Add the onion, and all pepper strips. Cook for 3–4 minutes, until slightly softened. If your skillet is too small, you will need to cook the chicken, remove it to a bowl, and then sauté the vegetables.

Warm the flour tortillas, covered with a paper towel, in the microwave for 20 seconds.

Place the warm tortillas on your work surface. Divide the chicken and sautéed vegetables among them.

Top each fajita with a dollop of nondairy sour cream, a sprinkle of cilantro leaves, and a splash of lime juice. Fold the sides of each fajita into the center to loosely enclose the filling.

This is one of my favorite meals and my kids love it too! And why not? I usually serve it with guacamole and a bag of tortilla chips. It is super-fast, easy, and a real crowd-pleaser.

kickin' chicken

Status: Meat

Prep Time: 5 minutes

Cook Time: 1 hr. 30 min.

Yield: 6–8 servings

2 chickens, cut into eighths

2 cups duck sauce

1 (1.25-ounce) packet taco seasoning packet, such as Ortega brand

Preheat oven to 350°F. Place the chicken pieces in single layers, skin-side-up, into two 9- by 13-inch baking pans.

In a medium bowl, whisk the duck sauce with the seasoning packet. Pour over the chicken pieces and massage to coat.

Bake, uncovered, for 1 hour and 30 minutes or until chicken is fully cooked and no longer pink, or a meat thermometer inserted into the thickest part of the thigh reads 180°F.

Transfer to a serving platter.

For REALLY kickin' chicken, turn up the heat. Two tablespoons of hot sauce, such as Frank's or Tabasco, added into the duck-sauce mixture will add more fire.

MEAT

rib steak au poivre

Status: Meat

Prep Time: 5 minutes

Cook Time: 30 minutes

Yield: 6 servings

6 (1-inch) rib steaks

fine sea salt

¼ cup rainbow peppercorns or peppercorn medley

2 tablespoons olive oil

1½ cups brandy

6 tablespoons vermouth

6 tablespoons Coco Lopez cream of coconut, from a small can

Season both sides of each rib steak with salt.

Place the peppercorns into a heavy-duty sandwich-or quart-sized Ziploc bag. Using a meat mallet, rolling pin, or hammer, crush the peppercorns to a medium to small grain.

With your palm, press the peppercorns into both sides of each steak for an even coating.

Heat the olive oil in a large skillet over medium heat. When it is hot, add the steaks, allowing them to sear for 6–8 minutes per side for medium-rare; do not move them around once you place them in the pan.

After the steaks are cooked, remove them to a platter; keep warm. Pour off the fat from the pan. With the heat off, add the brandy and vermouth. Carefully turn the heat to medium-low to avoid flaming the alcohol.

Add the Coco Lopez, swirling to pick up the flavors in the pan. Simmer for 7–10 minutes to thicken slightly.

Pour over the steaks. Serve warm.

Being short on time should not count you out of restaurant-quality steakhouse dinners. Bring the restaurant right to your kitchen and become your own 5-star chef with this winner. For the adventurous, try this with buffalo steaks. A very healthy alternative to beef, buffalo steaks may retain a very red color, even after being cooked to medium-rare; this is a result of the buffalo's diet and how little fat there is in the steaks.

This traditional French recipe gets it name from the coating of "poivre," or peppercorns. If you don't like the heat, coat the steaks lightly with the crushed peppercorns or coat only one side.

Peppercorn medleys are usually made up of whole black, pink, green, and white peppercorns, plus allspice.

panko-crusted filet split with melted leek sauce

Status: Meat

Prep Time: 10 minutes

Cook Time: 20 minutes

Yield: 6 servings

1 tablespoon Dijon mustard

1 teaspoon Worcestershire sauce (see note, page 59)

½ teaspoon garlic powder

½ teaspoon fine sea salt

2 pounds filet split or London broil

1 cup panko bread crumbs

1 tablespoon olive oil

2 tablespoons margarine

4 cloves fresh garlic, minced

5 leeks, white and pale green part only, washed well and very thinly sliced

1 cup chicken stock

½ cup white wine

¼ cup nondairy whipping cream, such as Richwhip brand

fine sea salt

¼ teaspoon freshly ground black pepper

In a small bowl, combine the mustard, Worcestershire sauce, garlic powder, and ½ teaspoon salt.

Brush this mixture onto both sides of the filet split or London broil. Pat on the panko bread crumbs to coat one side.

Heat the olive oil in a large skillet over medium heat. When the oil is hot, add the steak, crumb-side-up, and cook for 12 minutes. Flip the steak over and cook for 8 minutes longer for a perfect medium. Do not move the steak around once it hits the pan.

Meanwhile, prepare the sauce: Melt the margarine in a small pot over medium heat. Add the garlic and sliced leeks. Cook for 6–7 minutes until the leeks are very soft. Add the chicken stock and wine and cook for 5 minutes. Stir in the nondairy whipping cream. Season with salt and pepper.

Allow the filet to rest for 10 minutes to allow the juices to settle back in the center. Thinly slice on the diagonal. Transfer to plates or a platter. Drizzle melted-leek sauce over the slices.

Minute steaks are small steaks that have a tendon running through them. They are not my favorite cut. However, the butcher can take that same cut of meat and cut horizontally, above and below the tendon, removing it, and the result is two fabulous, large, trimmed pieces of meat, similar to London broil. Some butchers call it filet split others call it minute steak roast. It is excellent for grilling or pan searing. A quick 10 minutes per side will yield a perfect medium-rare.

chili dogs

Status: Meat

Prep Time: 5 minutes

Cook Time: 30 minutes

Yield: 6 servings

1 tablespoon olive oil

1 onion, cut into ¼-inch dice

2 teaspoons garlic powder

2 teaspoons chili powder

½ teaspoon fine sea salt

½ teaspoon paprika

⅛ teaspoon cayenne pepper

1 pound ground beef

1 (6-ounce) can tomato paste

1 (12-ounce) can beer, such as Coors Light

1 (15-ounce) can red kidney beans, drained and rinsed

6 hot dogs, grilled, or cooked in a grill pan or skillet

6 hoagie rolls

½ small onion, cut into ¼-inch dice, for garnish

Heat the oil in a medium pot over medium heat. Add the onion and sauté until shiny and translucent, about 4–5 minutes.

In a small bowl or measuring cup, combine the garlic powder, chili powder, salt, paprika, and cayenne pepper. Swirl or stir to combine.

Add the ground beef to the pan. Break up the chunks of beef with a wooden spoon.

When the meat is just starting to brown, add half the spice mixture. Cook for 2 minutes. Add the tomato paste. Fill the tomato paste can halfway with water and add the water. Stir to combine. Pour in the beer and mix again.

Add the kidney beans and half the remaining spice mixture. Simmer, uncovered, for 10 minutes. Add the rest of the spice mixture. Simmer for a final 5 minutes to cook the alcohol out of the beer. The beef should be cooked through so that no pink remains.

Spoon the chili over hot dogs in hoagie rolls and garnish with diced onion.

This chili recipe stands alone as a sensational rendition of a classic American dish. I make it often and serve it with a side of tortilla chips and rice or rolled into flour tortillas with a large salad. Adding the twist of hot dogs to make chili dogs turns it into a real family-friendly crowd pleaser.

The adding of spices to chili is what sets it apart as a food worthy of fairs, contests, and long-running family feuds. While chili makers keep their spice combinations secret, they all use a method called "dumping." The spices are mixed and added in batches, or "dumps," throughout the cooking process. In this way darker flavor nuances of the well-cooked spices mingle with the brighter high notes of the less-cooked ones.

Select a cheap light-bodied beer that won't overpower the chili.

Kosher by Design Short on Time

MEAT

gyros with tzatziki

Status: Meat

Prep Time: 10 minutes

Cook Time: 15 minutes

Yield: 6 servings

2½ pounds lamb shoulder chops or 2 pounds cubed lamb; trim any bones

2 teaspoons schwarma spice, such as the Pereg brand

1-2 tablespoons extra-virgin olive oil, divided

½ English (hothouse) cucumber, peeled, cut into 3 pieces

1 teaspoon chopped fresh mint leaves

½ cup nondairy sour cream, such as Tofutti brand

3 large pita breads

½ head romaine lettuce, shredded

1 beefsteak tomato, chopped

Trim the lamb chops: Cut around the bone and cartilage, slicing off any meat. If using the lamb cubes, slice them into strips. Place the sliced lamb into a medium bowl. Toss with the spice mixture and 1 tablespoon of extra-virgin olive oil to combine.

Heat a large nonstick skillet over medium heat. (If your skillet is not nonstick, coat it with 1 tablespoon of olive oil.) When the skillet is hot, add the spiced lamb in a single layer. Cook for 3 minutes. Use tongs to turn each piece and cook for 2–3 minutes on the other side, until cooked through. Add more olive oil as necessary if cooking in batches.

Prepare the tzatziki: In the bowl of a food processor fitted with a metal blade, chop the cucumber and mint with a few quick pulses. This can also be done in a quart-sized container using an immersion blender. Mix this into the nondairy sour cream. Set aside.

Slice each pita in half. Warm the pitas in the oven or microwave. Fill them with the shredded lettuce, chopped tomatoes, grilled lamb, and a dollop of tzatziki sauce.

Gyros are one of those great New York City vendor foods that fill the streets with fabulous aromas. New Yorkers call them gyros, authentic Greeks pronounce them "yehros." Either way, they make a delicious quick meal. Traditionally, tzatziki is a cooling yogurt sauce that tops gyros to play off the spiciness. This parve version does just that.

Using the shoulder chops is a little more work but will yield a more tender result. If you don't have lamb you can substitute strips of boneless, skinless chicken breast.

If you can't find the Pereg schwarma spice, make a mixture composed of 1 teaspoon each of the following spices: paprika, garlic powder, allspice, cayenne pepper, cumin, and ground clove. You will need 2 teaspoons for this recipe. Store any extra in an old spice bottle or a baby food jar.

Kosher by Design Short on Time
MEAT

apricot-teriyaki-glazed roast beef and vegetables

Status: Meat

Prep Time: 10 minutes

Cook Time: 2-2½ hours

Yield: 6–8 servings

2 acorn squash, with skin, seeded and cut into 2-inch chunks

2 large sweet potatoes, with skin, cut into 2-inch chunks

1 cup fresh or frozen cranberries

1 large red onion, cut into chunks

¼ cup olive oil

½ teaspoon fine sea salt

4-5 pound silver tip roast beef or rib eye roast, washed and patted dry

1 (12-ounce) jar good-quality apricot preserves, such as the Hero or Sarabeth brands

¼ cup teriyaki sauce

1 tablespoon yellow mustard

¼ teaspoon ground ginger

Preheat oven to 400°F. Place the acorn squash and sweet potato chunks into a large roasting pan. Sprinkle on the cranberries and scatter the chunks of red onion. Drizzle the vegetables with olive oil and salt.

Place the roast beef on top of the vegetables; do not use a rack.

In a medium bowl, whisk the apricot preserves, teriyaki, mustard, and ginger. Pour over the top of the meat, allowing the sauce to run down over the sides.

Roast, uncovered, for 30 minutes. Reduce the heat to 350°F. Bake for 1½-2 hours or until desired degree of doneness. Allow the meat to stand for 15 minutes before slicing to allow the juices to settle back into the center.

Serve with the vegetables.

The key to a great roast, in both taste and texture, is learning not to overcook it. Meat should be cooked to a perfect medium, 138°F. Any meat will continue to cook and its internal temperature will increase 5-10 degrees, after being removed from the oven and this is where the danger of overcooking comes in. Use a meat thermometer for perfect results every time. Insert it 2-inches into the center or thickest part of the meat and never let it touch any bone. If the meat's internal temperature on removal from the oven rises above 138°F, the result will be tougher and drier meat.

mandarin orange beef

Status: Meat

Prep Time: 10 minutes

Cook Time: 15 minutes

Yield: 6–8 servings

1 (15-ounce) can mandarin oranges, drained, juice reserved

zest and juice of 2 navel oranges

2 teaspoons cornstarch

2-3 tablespoons olive oil

2 carrots, sliced in half lengthwise and then cut into half-moons

6 ounces snow peas, ends trimmed, each sliced in half

2 green bell peppers, seeded and thinly sliced into short strips

2½ pounds skirt steak, thinly sliced on the diagonal

6 cloves fresh garlic, chopped

5-6 scallions, thinly sliced on the diagonal

4 teaspoons teriyaki sauce

Pour the juice from the can of mandarin oranges into a medium bowl, reserving the oranges. After zesting the navel oranges, squeeze their juice into the bowl of mandarin orange juice. Remove 2 tablespoons and combine with the cornstarch in a small bowl. Stir to dissolve and set aside.

In a very large skillet, heat the oil over medium heat. (If you only have a 10-inch skillet or smaller, you will need to cook the meat and then the vegetables in batches, and then combine.) Add the sliced steak and sauté for 5 minutes. Pour off excess juices. Turn the slices and add the carrots, snow peas, and green bell pepper. Sauté for 3 minutes. Add the orange juice. Heat through.

Add the garlic, orange zest, and cornstarch mixture. Bring to a simmer.

Add the scallions and teriyaki sauce. Toss the meat and vegetables.

Remove to a platter and top with mandarin oranges.

I like serving this dish over sesame noodles. My favorite recipe for this is on page 27 of the original Kosher by Design, and I recommend you try it for a treat your family will love. It goes well over rice, too.

blackened veal chops with black-eyed pea ragout

Status: Meat

Prep Time: 10 minutes

Cook Time: 20 minutes

Yield: 6 servings

3 tablespoons olive oil, divided

¼ cup blackening or Cajun-spice mix, plus extra for ragout

6 (1-inch thick) veal chops with bone

2 large bunches Swiss red chard

3 cloves fresh garlic, minced

2 plum tomatoes, chopped

1 (15.5-ounce) can black-eyed peas, drained and rinsed

fine sea salt

freshly ground black pepper

Preheat the broiler.

In a small bowl mix 2 tablespoons of the oil with the blackening or Cajun spice. Brush it on both sides of the veal chops, coating all surfaces. Place the veal chops in a single layer on a broiler pan. Broil 6 inches from the heat for 7–9 minutes per side for medium.

While the chops are cooking, prepare the ragout: Slice off and discard the root end of the Swiss chard. You can also trim off the stems, leaving a few inches below the leaves. It is okay to leave some of the stem for texture in the ragout. Wash the leaves carefully, as they contain a lot of dirt and grit. Chop the leaves. Heat the remaining tablespoon of olive oil in a large pot over medium-high heat. Add the Swiss chard and garlic. Sauté for 5 minutes, stirring occasionally, until the garlic is fragrant but not browned.

Add the chopped tomatoes and the black-eyed peas. Cook for 3–4 minutes.

Season with salt, a large pinch of blackening or Cajun spice, and freshly ground black pepper.

Transfer the ragout to the center of a large bowl. Stand the veal chops up, leaning them against the ragout.

When I think of Southern cooking I generally think of comfort foods, such as long-simmering soups and stews, Southern fried chicken, and lots of greens served up with a side of warmth and hospitality.

Greens such as collard, turnip, mustard, and chard grow in profusion in the South and are a staple of that cooking. This distinctive dish mixes greens with veal chops and black-eyed peas for a gorgeous and healthful dinner plate that requires nothing on the side.

moroccan hamburgers

Status: Meat

Prep Time: 10 minutes

Cook Time: 10 minutes

Yield: 6 servings

2 pounds ground beef or ground lamb

1 teaspoon dried oregano

1 teaspoon ground coriander

1 teaspoon fine sea salt

1 teaspoon freshly ground black pepper

1 teaspoon paprika

1 teaspoon cayenne pepper

2 pinches of crushed red pepper flakes

2-3 tablespoons olive oil

½ English (hothouse) cucumber, thinly sliced

½ red onion, cut into thin slices

1½ tablespoons apple-cider vinegar

½ cup mayonnaise

1 tablespoon chopped fresh mint leaves

6 hamburger buns

Place the ground meat into a medium bowl. Add the oregano, ground coriander, salt, black pepper, paprika, cayenne pepper, and red pepper flakes. Mix well. Form into 6 patties.

Heat a grill pan or medium skillet over medium-high heat. Add the oil and heat until almost smoking. Add the patties and cook 5 minutes per side. Try not to move the burgers around so you will get nice grill marks and a good sear. Re-oil the pan as necessary if working in batches.

Meanwhile, place the thinly sliced cucumber and red onions into a medium bowl. Toss with the vinegar and allow to stand for a few minutes.

In a small bowl, mix the chopped mint into the mayonnaise. Set aside.

When you remove the burgers from the pan, place the buns, cut-side down, into the pan. This will toast them and at the same time they will pick up nice flavor.

Spread both sides of the toasted buns with the minted mayonnaise. Top each Moroccan burger with a few slices of the cucumber and red onion.

The history of Morocco is reflected in its food, which has a true multicultural flavor. As people from other countries passed though the region, they introduced their cultures' cooking techniques and ingredients. Abundant spices play an important role in rich flavors and aromatic Moroccan cooking.

lamb chops with parsley pesto

Status: Meat
Prep Time: 5 minutes
Cook Time: 10 minutes
Yield: 6 servings

2 cloves fresh garlic
1 teaspoon fine sea salt
1 teaspoon dried rosemary
¼ teaspoon ground cayenne pepper
1 cup loosely packed fresh mint leaves

1 cup loosely packed fresh parsley leaves
1 tablespoon plus 1 teaspoon lemon juice (can be bottled)
½ cup olive oil
18 baby lamb chops

Preheat the broiler to high.

In the bowl of food processor fitted with a metal blade, pulse the garlic, salt, and rosemary. Add the cayenne pepper, mint leaves, parsley leaves, and lemon juice. Pulse. With the machine running, slowly pour in the olive oil and allow the mixture to fully combine.

With a flexible spatula, transfer one-third of the pesto to a small bowl and reserve for serving after the chops are cooked. Pour the rest into a second bowl.

Place the lamb chops on a broiler pan. Lightly brush both sides of the lamb chops with the pesto.

Broil the lamb chops, 6–8 inches from the heat, for 7 minutes. Turn the lamb chops over and broil for another 3 minutes.

To serve, place 3 lamb chops on each plate with a dollop of the reserved parsley pesto.

This delicious green sauce can just as easily go over sliced steak or chicken, but the hints of mint, garlic, and rosemary really complement lamb beautifully. If you have a mini-food processor, it will work even better than a full-sized one to really grind the ingredients to a good, thick paste.

stuffed veal roast

Status: Meat

Prep Time: 10 minutes

Cook Time: 1 hr. 30 min.

Yield: 6 servings

5 medium white button mushrooms

½ (10-ounce) box frozen chopped spinach, defrosted

3 sprigs fresh rosemary

10 ounces large pimiento-stuffed green olives

zest of 1 orange

zest of 1 small lemon

1 (3-pound) veal roast, netted and tied

2 tablespoons olive oil

3-4 tablespoons thick honey-mustard, such as the Honeycup brand

Preheat oven to 375°F.

Place the mushrooms, the ½-box defrosted spinach, leaves from the rosemary sprigs, olives, orange zest, and lemon zest into the bowl of a food processor fitted with a metal blade. Pulse to combine to a paste.

Untie the roast. Season both sides with salt and pepper. Spread the stuffing paste evenly over the surface of the veal, generously covering it.

Reroll the roast and tie it just tightly enough to secure; don't tie too tightly or the filling will all ooze out. The filling will be visible.

Heat the olive oil in a large skillet. Add the veal roast and sear on all sides until the meat is a deep golden-brown.

Place the seared roast into a roasting pan. Rub all the surfaces with a thick coating of the honey-mustard. Bake for 1 hour and 15–20 minutes. Allow the roast to stand for 10 minutes before slicing. The roast should be juicy and slightly pink in the center.

This show-stopping presentation is for wowing guests when you only have a few minutes to prep and get something into the oven. Make sure you have butcher's twine on hand for tying the roast.

wine-braised brisket with tomatoes

Status: Meat

Prep Time: 15 minutes

Cook Time: 2½ hours

Yield: 6–8 servings

2 tablespoons olive oil

3-4 pound brisket

  fine sea salt

  freshly ground black pepper

1 (28-ounce) can diced tomatoes

2 plum tomatoes, coarsely chopped

2 medium onions, cut into ¼-inch dice

4 ounces crimini mushrooms, sliced

1½ cups Merlot, Cabernet Sauvignon, or other red wine

Preheat oven to 350°F.

In a large ovenproof pot, heat the oil over medium heat. Season the brisket on both sides with salt and pepper.

Place into the pot and sear on both sides, about 5–7 minutes per side, or until browned.

Add the diced tomatoes, chopped plum tomatoes, onions, and mushrooms. Pour the wine into the pot to just cover the meat; some of the tomatoes will not be covered.

Cover the pot and transfer to the oven. Cook for 2½ hours or until the meat is cooked and tender. Remove from oven.

When the meat is cooled, transfer to a cutting board, reserving the vegetables in the pot. Thinly slice the meat across the grain. Return the meat to the pot and heat through with the vegetable mixture.

Transfer to a serving platter.

My 5-year-old friend and food critic Ezra Finklestein came for a midweek dinner. Later, when his mom was halfway home, he asked if they were closer to their house or my house. She asked why, assuming it was a bathroom request, but instead he pronounced that this brisket was "the bestest meat he ever had!" and he wanted to go back for more. I hope your kids will feel the same.

mexican lasagne

Status: Meat

Prep Time: 15 minutes

Cook Time: 30 minutes

Yield: 12 servings

¼ cup canola or olive oil

1 Spanish onion, cut into ¼-inch dice

1 green bell pepper, seeded and cut into ¼-inch dice

2½ pounds ground beef

1 (1.25-ounce) packet taco seasoning

6 (10-inch) flour tortillas or more if you are using smaller flour tortillas

1 (15-ounce) can refried pinto or kidney beans

2 (28-ounce) cans crushed tomatoes

1 (8-ounce) container nondairy cream cheese, such as Tofutti brand

5-6 scallions, chopped

3 tablespoons chopped fresh cilantro

Preheat oven to 350°F. Spray a large (9- by 13-inch) rectangular oven-to-table baking dish with nonstick cooking spray.

Heat the oil in a large skillet over medium heat. Add the onion and green bell pepper. Sauté for 6 minutes or until vegetables are softened.

Add the ground beef and use a wooden spoon to break up the chunks of beef. Mix in the taco seasoning. Sauté until the meat is no longer pink. Remove from heat.

Spread 3–4 heaping tablespoons of the refried beans into a thin layer on one side of each tortilla. Cut each tortilla in half.

Place 4 tortilla halves, plain-side-down, into the prepared pan. Place the straight edges against the short edges of the baking pan so that they fill the bottom of the pan better. Overlap the two center tortillas as necessary in the middle.

Spread one-third of the meat mixture evenly over the refried beans.

Spread 1½ cups crushed tomatoes over the meat.

Measure 3 tablespoons of the nondairy cream cheese and break into small pieces. Scatter the pieces of cream cheese over the tomatoes.

Sprinkle with one-third of the chopped scallions and a sprinkle of cilantro.

Repeat layering in this order 2 more times

Bake, uncovered, for 15 minutes. Serve hot.

Looking for a delicious, flavorful, lower-carb option to a meat lasagne? Look no further! This dish can easily be assembled the night before and kept covered in the refrigerator. Just uncover and heat when you are ready to serve.

The Eden organic company makes cans of plain refried beans as well as spicy ones. Experiment with both to see which you like better.

bloody-mary-marinated london broil

Status: Meat

Prep Time: 10 minutes

Cook Time: 20 minutes

Yield: 6 servings

1 large shoulder London broil, about 3 pounds

1 cup tomato juice

1 tablespoon lemon juice

1 tablespoon lime juice

1 tablespoon prepared white horseradish

1 tablespoon Worcestershire sauce (see note, page 59)

2 cloves fresh garlic, minced

2 dashes hot sauce, such as Tabasco or Frank's Red Hot

½ teaspoon celery salt

½ teaspoon dried oregano

½ teaspoon fine sea salt

½ teaspoon freshly ground black pepper

olive oil

Score the meat on both sides, making shallow diamond-shaped cuts. Set the meat into a shallow non-reactive baking dish such as Pyrex or glass.

In a medium bowl, whisk the tomato juice, lemon juice, lime juice, horseradish, Worcestershire sauce, garlic, hot sauce, celery salt, oregano, salt, and black pepper.

Pour the marinade over the meat and let stand at room temperature.

Meanwhile, grease a barbecue grill or grill pan lightly with olive oil and preheat it.

Remove the meat from the marinade, pouring the marinade into a small pot, and sear the meat for 10 minutes per side.

Meanwhile heat the marinade over medium heat. Bring to a simmer for 3–5 minutes until slightly thickened.

Allow the meat 10 minutes to rest. Thinly slice on the diagonal. Serve the slices with the sauce on the side or drizzled over the top.

A Bloody Mary is a famous cocktail containing vodka, tomato juice, and other spices and flavorings. Bartenders may guard their secret recipes, but most garnish the drinks with stalks of celery. It is one of the few cocktails that is enjoyed at a brunch table. This recipe takes the non-alcoholic ingredients of a traditional Bloody Mary and turns them into a fabulous marinade and sauce for steak.

kalamata-mushroom meat sauce

Status: Meat

Prep Time: 10 minutes

Cook Time: 25 minutes

Yield: 6–8 servings

2 tablespoons olive oil

1 small onion, cut into ¼-inch dice

1½ teaspoons dried basil

½ teaspoon dried oregano

½ teaspoon dried rosemary

1 red bell pepper, seeded and cut into ¼-inch dice

1 pound ground beef

1 (28-ounce) can diced tomatoes

1 (6-ounce) can tomato paste

3 fresh garlic cloves, minced

6 ounces crimini mushrooms, thinly sliced

5 ounces Kalamata olives, pitted, chopped

mafalda or other pasta shape, cooked al dente according to package directions or crusty bread such as French or Italian bread

Heat the olive oil in a large pot over medium heat. Add the onion and sauté for 3–4 minutes until it is shiny and translucent. Stir the basil, oregano, and rosemary into the onions. Cook until the spices are aromatic, 2–3 minutes.

Add the red bell pepper and the ground beef. Use a wooden spoon to break up the meat.

Add the tomatoes, tomato paste, and garlic. Simmer for 10 minutes, stirring to keep breaking up the meat.

Add the mushrooms and simmer for 5 minutes. Add the olives. Heat through.

Serve over pasta or with crusty bread.

To pit the olives, just press them with your palm; the pit will pop right out. This is a great job for the kids.

FISH & PASTA

lacquered salmon

Status: Parve

Prep Time: 5 minutes

Cook Time: 25 minutes

Yield: 6 servings

½ cup soy sauce

½ cup sugar

½ teaspoon ground ginger

2 cloves fresh garlic, minced

2 teaspoons Jack Daniels or other whiskey

olive oil

6 (6-ounce) salmon fillets

fine sea salt

freshly ground black pepper

1 (5-ounce) can crushed pineapple, drained

Preheat oven to 375°F.

Place the soy sauce and sugar into a medium pot. Bring to a boil. Add the ginger, garlic, and whiskey. Reduce the heat to low and simmer for 5 minutes. Remove half the sauce to a container to drizzle over the fish after it is cooked. Set aside. The sauce can be made in advance and rewarmed to make it pourable.

Brush a broiling pan with olive oil.

Season the salmon fillets with salt and pepper. Place them on the prepared pan. Sprinkle 1 tablespoon of crushed pineapple over each fillet. Drizzle 1 tablespoon of the soy sauce mixture over the top of each fillet.

Bake, uncovered, for about 20–25 minutes, until the salmon is pink and slightly firm to the touch.

Drizzle with the reserved sauce before serving.

Wonderful Asian flavors come together in this dish in a sauce that also relies on a little American whiskey. The salmon is great with a side salad or mashed potatoes.

roasted lemon-pepper cod

Status: Dairy

Prep Time: 5 minutes

Cook Time: 20 minutes

Yield: 6 servings

6 (6-ounce) cod fillets

fine sea salt

2 lemons

cracked black pepper, or coarsely
ground black pepper

2 cups heavy cream

1 teaspoon onion powder

¼ cup sour cream

Preheat the oven to 375°F. Line a jelly roll pan with parchment paper.

Season both sides of each cod fillet with salt. Place them onto prepared pan.

Using a microplane, zest the lemons over the fish, reserving the lemons. Sprinkle with black pepper.

Roast for 20 minutes.

Meanwhile, pour the cream into a medium pot. Heat over medium heat until the cream starts to form bubbles around the rim. Reduce the heat to medium-low. Add the juice from the lemons and the onion powder. Simmer over low heat for 7–10 minutes to reduce in volume and until slightly thickened.

Remove the pot from the heat and whisk in the sour cream and any fish juices from the pan.

Transfer the fish to plates or a platter. Spoon the sauce over the fish.

Try this recipe with other thick white firm-fleshed fish such as halibut or grouper. If preparing the sauce in advance, add a little milk to smooth the sauce while reheating.

cornmeal-crusted flounder with tartar sauce

Status: Parve

Prep Time: 10 minutes

Cook Time: 10 minutes

Yield: 6 servings

CORNMEAL-CRUSTED FLOUNDER:

6 large flounder or sole fillets

fine sea salt

freshly ground black pepper

1 cup all-purpose flour

2 large eggs, lightly beaten with 2 tablespoons water

1 cup ground yellow cornmeal

3 tablespoons olive oil, plus more if needed

TARTAR SAUCE:

1 cup mayonnaise

2 sour pickles, very finely chopped

1 teaspoon Worcestershire sauce

1 teaspoon hot sauce, such as Tabasco

Cut each fillet on either side of the spine and remove the spine; you will be left with 2 long pieces of flounder from each fillet.

Season both sides of each piece of fish with salt and pepper.

Arrange 3 bowls on your work surface.

Place the flour in one bowl, the beaten egg in the second bowl, and the cornmeal in the third bowl.

Take the fish, one piece a time. Dip it into the flour; shaking off the excess. Dip it into the egg; shaking off the excess, and then dip it into the cornmeal, shaking off the excess. Repeat with the remaining 11 pieces.

Heat the olive oil in a large skillet over medium heat. When the oil is hot, but not smoking, add the fish in a single layer, working in batches if necessary. Cook for 4 minutes per side, or until a crisp crust forms and the fish is slightly firm to the touch. Remove to a plate or platter. If you are doing this in batches you will need more oil.

Meanwhile, prepare the tartar sauce: In a small bowl whisk together the mayonnaise, pickles, Worcestershire sauce, and hot sauce.

Serve the fish with the tartar sauce.

For a great sandwich, pile these kid-friendly fillets into hoagie rolls with some lettuce, tomato, and tartar sauce. You can choose any mild-flavored fish that's locally available and in season; cod, halibut, or grouper are good choices. Serve with a side of any kind of slaw for a complete meal. Feel free to spice this dish up by mixing 1 tablespoon blackening spice into the cornmeal before you coat the fish.

phyllo confetti halibut

Status: Parve

Prep Time: 10 minutes

Cook Time: 20 minutes

Yield: 6 servings

nonstick cooking spray, preferably olive-oil flavor

1 box phyllo (fillo) dough, defrosted

6 (6-8 ounce) halibut fillets

fine sea salt

freshly ground black pepper

2 tablespoons thick honey-mustard, such as Honeycup brand

⅓ cup loosely packed fresh parsley, finely chopped

2 pints grape or cherry tomatoes, each cut in half

1 tablespoon extra-virgin olive oil

3 cloves fresh garlic, minced

Preheat oven to 375°F. Spray a baking dish with nonstick olive-oil spray.

Remove the phyllo dough from the box. Remove the outer plastic bag from the phyllo dough. Keeping it in a roll, use a serrated knife to cut 2-inches off the end. Return the rest to the refrigerator and reserve it for another use.

Gently remove the inner plastic sheet. Re-roll the stack of dough, and, with a serrated knife, shred the dough into thin strips. Fluff out the strips with your hands.

Season the halibut fillets with salt and pepper. Spread an even layer of honey-mustard on each fillet. Place fillets in a single layer into prepared baking dish.

Arrange the shreds of phyllo dough over each fillet. Sprinkle with parsley.

Generously spray the nonstick olive-oil spray over the top of the fish.

Toss the tomatoes with the olive oil and minced garlic. Add to the baking dish.

Bake, uncovered, for 15–20 minutes, depending on the thickness of the fish, until the phyllo is light golden-brown, and the fish is white and slightly firm to the touch.

Transfer to plates or a platter.

Halibut has a mild flavor and a wonderful flaky texture. It is great broiled, baked, or grilled.

The shredded phyllo dough dresses it up in a flash so it appears far more complicated than it is. Easy and delicious!

yellowfin tuna with citrus-hoisin sauce

Status: Parve

Prep Time: 5 minutes

Cook Time: 5 minutes

Yield: 6 servings

1 tablespoon olive oil

6 (6-ounce) yellowfin or ahi tuna steaks

fine sea salt

freshly ground black pepper

1 cup hoisin sauce

⅓ cup orange juice or mango nectar

2 tablespoons lime juice

leaves from 12 sprigs cilantro

3 scallions, thinly sliced on the diagonal

3 tablespoons dry-roasted peanuts, coarsely chopped

pinch of cayenne pepper

Heat the olive oil in a large skillet over medium heat. Season the tuna steaks with salt and pepper. When the oil is hot, sear the steaks for 1–2 minutes per side for medium-rare. Remove from skillet and set aside.

In a small bowl, whisk together the hoisin sauce, orange juice, and lime juice. Taste and season with salt as needed.

Slice the tuna into thin slices on the diagonal. Fan the slices out on each plate. Drizzle with some of the sauce.

Pile some of the cilantro and sliced scallions in the center of each plate. Scatter the peanuts over the fish.

Season with salt and a pinch of cayenne pepper.

Hoisin sauce, which is sold in jars in the Asian section of the supermarket, is both a condiment and a glaze used by the Chinese for meats and duck and is also good with fish. It is best known, perhaps, for its use in the famous dish, Peking Duck. Both spicy and sweet, hoisin is made of soybeans, garlic, sugar, vinegar, and spices. An open bottle can keep for months in the refrigerator.

tuna croquettes

Status: Parve

Prep Time: 5 minutes

Cook Time: 10 minutes

Yield: 8 servings

2 (12-ounce) cans solid white tuna in water, drained

⅔ cup unsalted matzo meal

¼ cup mayonnaise

4 large eggs

½ teaspoon garlic powder

½ teaspoon onion powder

½ teaspoon dried minced onion

½ teaspoon fine sea salt

2 tablespoons canola oil

In a medium-sized bowl, mix the tuna with the matzo meal, mayonnaise, eggs, garlic powder, onion powder, minced onion, and salt. Form 8 patties.

Heat the canola oil in a large skillet. When the oil is hot, place the patties into the pan in a single layer, working in batches if necessary, and fry for 3–4 minutes per side until golden-brown.

Remove to plates or a platter.

On the nights I work, my husband Kal takes over dinner duty. This is one of his famous kid-friendly dishes. My family loves it with spaghetti in ketchup. Kal claims that over the years he has had many requests from other cookbook authors asking him to share this recipe and until now has always refused. We should really appreciate his generosity in handing over this keeper.

almond-crusted sole with strawberry-mango salsa

Status: Dairy or Parve

Prep Time: 10 minutes

Cook Time: 10 minutes

Yield: 6 servings

ALMOND-CRUSTED SOLE:

olive oil

12 sole fillets

fine sea salt

freshly ground black pepper

1 cup slivered almonds

¼ cup panko bread crumbs

4 tablespoons butter or margarine, microwaved for 15 seconds

STRAWBERRY-MANGO SALSA:

1 mango, cut into ¼-inch dice

12 strawberries, stemmed, cut into ¼-inch dice

2 tablespoons balsamic vinegar

1 tablespoon extra-virgin olive oil

1 shallot, minced

12 fresh mint leaves, thinly sliced, for garnish

Preheat oven to 350°F. Brush the broiler pan with olive oil. Season each sole fillet with salt and pepper.

Place the almonds into a tall container, such as an empty quart-sized container. Add ¼ teaspoon salt and ¼ teaspoon pepper. With an immersion blender, pulse the almonds. Don't grind them too fine; you want to leave some texture. Add the panko bread crumbs. Toss to mix. Mix the softened butter or margarine into the almonds to make a paste.

Place 2 fillets together, one on top of the other, and place on the prepared pan. You should have 6 double fillets.

Pat the almond crust on the top of each double fillet.

Place into the hot oven and bake for 10 minutes. Place under the broiler for 1 minute if you want to make the crust more golden in color.

Meanwhile prepare the salsa: In a medium bowl, toss the mango, strawberries, balsamic vinegar, olive oil, ¼ teaspoon salt, and shallot. Mix together.

Serve the fish with a scoop of the salsa and garnish with a sprinkle of mint.

This dish combines the quintessential summer flavors of strawberry and mango in a light salsa. When I make this dish, I always count on making extra salsa to serve warm as a light dessert over a scoop of dairy or parve vanilla or strawberry ice-cream.

potato-crusted snapper with mushroom sauce

Status: Dairy

Prep Time: 10 minutes

Cook Time: 20 minutes

Yield: 6 servings

6 (6-ounce) red snapper fillets, with skin

fine sea salt

freshly ground black pepper

2 cups mashed-potato flakes

3 tablespoons olive oil, divided

3 tablespoons butter, divided

1 shallot, thinly sliced

3 cloves fresh garlic, chopped

8 ounces assorted exotic mushrooms, such as oyster, shiitake caps, and crimini mushrooms, sliced

2 cups Pinot Grigio or other white wine

½ cup light cream

Season the snapper fillets with salt and pepper. Pour the mashed potato flakes into a plate. Dip the fish into the mashed potato flakes, pressing to get them to stick. Turn the fillets over and press the flakes into the skin side. Set fish aside.

Meanwhile, prepare the sauce: In a medium skillet, heat 1 tablespoon each of olive oil and butter over medium heat. Add the shallot and garlic; sauté for 4 minutes, or until shiny and translucent.

Add the mushrooms and cook for 2 minutes or until fragrant. Add the wine and bring to a simmer. Allow the wine to reduce for 6–7 minutes. Stir in the light cream. Keep warm.

Cook the fish: In a large skillet, heat 1 tablespoon each of the oil and butter. When the butter is melted and the oil is hot, add 2 or 3 pieces of fish, skin-side-up, in a single layer. Cook for 4–5 minutes or until the potatoes are golden-brown and crusted onto the fish. Flip and cook on the other side for 5 minutes or until cooked through.

Remove the fish to a platter. Wipe out the pan between batches. Add remaining tablespoon each of olive oil and butter to the pan. When hot, add the remaining snapper fillets. Cook as directed above.

Serve the fish with sauce.

This dish is always a hit at our table, even with my kids. Red snapper is a mild-tasting fish that, since it doesn't fall apart easily, is a breeze to cook. The potato crust is fabulous and could not be easier. The sauce just puts it over the top as a dish you might eat in any fine restaurant.

fettuccine alfredo

Status: Dairy

Prep Time: 5 minutes

Cook Time: 15 minutes

Yield: 6 servings

1 (16-ounce) box fettuccine pasta

1 tablespoon butter

2 cloves fresh garlic, minced

3 cups heavy cream

4 large egg yolks

2 teaspoons fine sea salt

¼ teaspoon freshly ground black pepper

2 pinches ground nutmeg

⅓ cup grated Parmesan cheese

Cook the pasta in a large pot of boiling heavily salted water until al dente, according to package directions. Drain, rinse under cold water to stop the cooking process, and toss with a drop of olive oil to prevent sticking.

While the pasta is cooking, melt the butter in a medium skillet over medium-low heat. Add the garlic and sauté for 3 minutes. Add the cream. Bring to a simmer over medium heat and cook for 5 minutes to reduce the cream by one-third.

Meanwhile, in a small bowl, whisk the egg yolks with the salt, pepper, and nutmeg.

Remove ½ cup of the hot cream mixture and mix it into the egg yolks to temper them so they do not scramble when you add them into the larger skillet of hot cream. Whisk the tempered yolks into the cream. Turn off the heat and whisk in the Parmesan.

Pour the Alfredo sauce over the pasta and toss together with tongs. Serve warm.

Fettuccine Alfredo is creamy and delicious and really must be served immediately or the sauce will thicken up considerably. When I know family member will be coming home for dinner at various times, I keep the sauce separate from the pasta and thin it with some milk as it reheats. Once it is smooth and creamy, I toss in the pasta.

baked spaghetti pie

Status: Dairy

Prep Time: 5 minutes

Cook Time: 40 minutes

Yield: 8 servings

1 (16-ounce) box spaghetti

⅔ cup Parmesan cheese

1 cup ricotta cheese

4 large eggs, lightly beaten

½ teaspoon dried basil

½ teaspoon dried oregano

½ teaspoon fine sea salt

½ teaspoon freshly ground black pepper

1 (26-ounce) jar marinara sauce

4 ounces shredded mozzarella

¼ cup bread crumbs

Preheat oven to 350°F. Spray a 9-inch springform pan with nonstick cooking spray. Set aside.

Cook the pasta in a large pot of boiling heavily salted water until al dente, according to package directions. Drain.

Transfer the drained spaghetti back into the pot. Mix in the Parmesan, ricotta, eggs, basil, oregano, salt, pepper, and marinara sauce.

Layer half the spaghetti into the prepared pan. Sprinkle with the mozzarella. Top with remaining spaghetti. Toss the bread crumbs over the top.

Bake, covered, for 30 minutes.

Release the spring on the pan. Slice and serve.

This dish is a welcome staple at every dairy family event my sister Karen has ever thrown. It is a great way to use up leftover spaghetti — and so good it's worth cooking up a fresh batch as well!

penne florentine à la vodka

Status: Dairy or Parve

Prep Time: 5 minutes

Cook Time: 20 minutes

Yield: 6–8 servings

1 (16-ounce) box penne pasta

3 tablespoons butter or margarine

1 onion, finely diced

1 clove fresh garlic, minced

½ teaspoon red-pepper flakes

1 cup vodka

1 (28-ounce) can tomato purée

1 cup heavy cream or ½ cup nondairy sour cream

½ teaspoon salt

2 cups firmly packed baby spinach leaves

½ cup grated Parmesan, optional for dairy meals

Cook the pasta in a large pot of boiling heavily salted water until al dente, according to package directions. Drain.

Meanwhile, prepare the sauce: Melt the butter or margarine in a large skillet over medium heat. Add the onion and cook until shiny and translucent, 4–5 minutes. If it is starts to brown, lower the heat. Add the garlic and cook for 1 minute. Season with the red pepper flakes.

Remove from the heat and carefully add the vodka. Return the pan to the heat and simmer for 3 minutes to cook off the alcohol.

Add the tomato purée. Mix well. Add the heavy cream or nondairy sour cream. Simmer for 5 minutes. Season with the salt. Add the spinach and cook until wilted, 1–2 minutes.

Toss the penne with the sauce. Sprinkle with the Parmesan, if using.

Penne à la vodka is a family favorite that my kids frequently order at restaurants. Happily, it is easy enough to make at home and with the addition of the spinach, it becomes a healthful dish. The parve version is outstanding and less caloric, so be sure to try it both ways.

I like this dish very spicy; if you do, too, up the amount of red-pepper flakes.

spaghetti à la checca

Status: Parve

Prep Time: 5 minutes

Cook Time: 10 minutes

Yield: 6–8 servings

1 (16-ounce) box spaghetti

5 plum tomatoes, seeded and cut into ¼-inch dice

¼ cup packed fresh basil leaves, stacked and thinly sliced

2 cloves fresh garlic, minced

1¼ cups extra-virgin olive oil

½ teaspoon fine sea salt, plus more to taste

¼ teaspoon freshly ground black pepper, plus more to taste

Cook the pasta in a large pot of boiling heavily salted water until al dente, according to package directions. Drain, rinse in cold water, and set aside.

While the pasta is cooking, place the chopped tomatoes, sliced basil, and minced garlic into a medium bowl. Add the olive oil to cover the tomatoes. Add the salt and pepper.

Place the spaghetti into a large serving bowl. Pour on the tomato mixture. Use tongs to mix well. Season with more salt and pepper as needed. Serve warm or at room temperature.

This fresh, simple dish brings you right to Italy's doorstep; just make sure you start with really good tomatoes. For a dairy twist add small cubes of hand-rolled mozzarella.

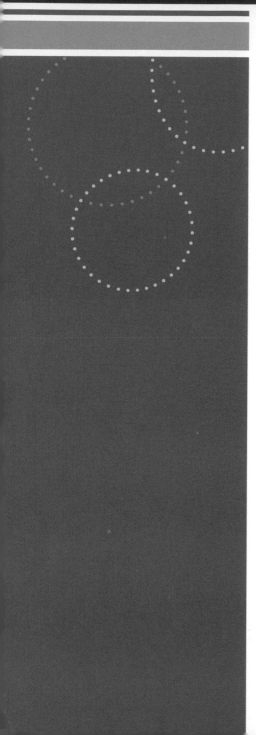

Although many people own slow cookers, very few use them for anything other than Shabbat cholent. For an appliance that yields remarkable results and is already taking up space in your kitchen, it is really underappreciated. Whether you spend the day out at work or just out of your house, there is nothing like coming home and being greeted by inviting smells of your waiting dinner.

Slow cookers, widely known as "crock pots," require a bit of pre-planning, but once the ingredients are in the pot, your work is done. These recipes go beyond the typical stews you would expect to find in such a section. I have included fancy-enough food, such as Lamb Shanks Cassoulet, so that you can even think of your slow cooker for entertaining.

Just a few tips for using a slow cooker: Use tough cuts of meat that benefit from moist gentle heat, like brisket or lamb shanks. Sear the meat or chicken in a skillet before adding it to the slow cooker. This boosts flavor and color. Use cut -up pieces of chicken on the bone, as boneless, skinless breasts will become too dry. Don't overcook chicken for the same reason, and make sure you use low heat for chicken. In adapting your own recipes for the slow cooker, halve the liquid. Liquid has no place to evaporate and will dilute the flavor of your food. Cooking beans in a slow cooker is a huge convenience, as there is no need to keep checking the water. Chili works well too. Avoid lifting the lid during the cooking process, as much heat is lost this way.

If you are buying one for the first time, purchase the biggest slow cooker you can get so you can make big batches of recipes. Slow-cooked food freezes well.

SLOW COOKER

mushroom barley soup

Status: Meat

Prep Time: 10 minutes

Cook Time: 5–8 hours

Yield: 6–8 servings

2 cups beef broth

8 cups good-quality chicken stock

½ cup baby carrots, cut into ½-inch rounds

2 stalks celery, thinly sliced

10 ounces white mushrooms, sliced

8 ounces crimini mushrooms, sliced

⅛ cup dried porcini mushrooms

2 tablespoons sherry or vermouth

1 teaspoon dried minced onion

1 teaspoon fine sea salt

¼ teaspoon dried thyme

¼ teaspoon dried fennel seed

¾ cup pearl barley, raw

Place the beef broth, chicken stock, carrots, celery, white mushrooms, crimini mushrooms, dried mushrooms, sherry, minced onion, salt, thyme, and fennel into the bowl of a slow cooker. Stir to mix all the ingredients. Add the barley. Cover and set on high for 5 hours or on low for 8 hours.

Ladle into a covered tureen or bowls.

To make this a full meal in a bowl, you can add beef flanken to the pot. Either way, this is a warm, hearty soup that you'll look forward to all day. Just knowing it's cooking while you work gives you a sense of well-being. For the beef broth, use homemade, canned, or dissolved bouillon powder.

mulligacholent

Status: Meat

Prep Time: 15 minutes

Cook Time: 7–8 hours

Yield: 8–10 servings

4 chicken thighs, bones and skin removed

½ cup dried chickpeas (garbanzo beans)

2 russet potatoes, peeled and cut into small cubes

1 large onion, chopped

2 cups baby carrots, chopped

2 stalks celery, thinly sliced

1 small Italian eggplant, peeled and cut into small cubes

1 cup frozen yellow corn

1 red bell pepper, seeded and chopped

½ cup raw, unsalted, shelled pistachio nuts

½ cup raw, unsalted cashew nuts

½ cup fresh Italian parsley, chopped

½ teaspoon curry powder

½ teaspoon freshly ground black pepper

pinch of ground marjoram

pinch of ground nutmeg

pinch of ground allspice

½ teaspoon dried thyme

½ teaspoon oregano

1 bay leaf

¼ cup Coco Lopez cream of coconut

¼ cup lime juice

1 cup tomato sauce

1 cup water

10 cups chicken stock

Place all the ingredients into the bowl of a slow cooker. Stir with a wooden spoon. Cook on a high setting, uncovered, for 7–8 hours, stirring occasionally if possible. It will reduce somewhat and thicken.

Remove bay leaf and discard it. Using an immersion blender right in the slow cooker, partially purée the soup, leaving some chunks of vegetables.

If you don't own a slow cooker, you can cook the soup in a large pot over medium-high heat, uncovered, for 4½ hours, stirring occasionally. Ladle into bowls.

Inspiration for this funky spin on mulligatawny soup, called Mulligacholent, goes to my creative sister-in-law Sarah. She came up with the idea to cook the soup in a crockpot. I had never used mine for anything but cholent and the thought of using it midweek intrigued me. It was the inspiration for this chapter!

Together with my brother-in-law Steven, and after a week of all mulligatawny all of the time, we worked out the kinks in this soup. It is rich, thick, aromatic, and completely satisfying.

Coco Lopez is canned, thickened, sweetened coconut milk that is usually used in mixed drinks. It is available in any supermarket.

pulled barbecue beef

Status: Meat

Prep Time: 10 minutes

Cook Time: 4-8 hours

Yield: 12 servings

3 pounds top of the brisket, top of the rib, or other fatty roast

fine sea salt

freshly ground black pepper

1-2 tablespoons canola oil

1 red onion, halved and very thinly sliced

2 tablespoons Worcestershire sauce (see note, page 59)

1 tablespoon Jack Daniels or other whiskey

1 teaspoon garlic powder

1 teaspoon onion powder

1 teaspoon dried thyme

4 cups chicken stock

1 (18-ounce) bottled barbecue sauce, such as KC Masterpiece brand

2 tablespoons cornstarch dissolved in 2 tablespoons water

12 crusty rolls

store-bought coleslaw, optional

Line the slow cooker with a liner bag if you have one. Most require a cup or two of water in the bottom of the crock before the bag is inserted.

Untie the shoulder roast. Open it and slice it into 2 pieces. Season each piece on both sides with salt and pepper.

Heat the oil in a large skillet over medium heat. Sear the meat on both sides. Place into the slow cooker. Sauté onion in the same skillet for 3 minutes, stirring to pick up the flavor and the browned bits of meat. Top the meat with the onions.

In a large bowl, mix the Worcestershire sauce, whisky, garlic powder, onion powder, thyme, and stock. Pour the stock mixture around the meat; try to keep the onions from being washed off. Pour the barbecue sauce directly onto the meat. Cover and cook on high for 4 hours, or on low for 8 hours, until done. The meat is ready when it easily pulls apart with a fork.

Remove meat from the slow cooker, reserving the sauce. Shred the meat by pulling in opposite directions with two forks.

Place meat into a bowl. Pour the sauce into a medium pot. Add the dissolved cornstarch and bring to a boil over medium heat. Boil until thickened, about 3 minutes. Pour the thickened gravy over the meat.

Pile the shredded meat on crusty rolls. Drizzle with some of the gravy and top with coleslaw. Cover with the tops of the rolls.

In a kitchen session with Chef Damian, I asked for help to make a real pulled barbecue sandwich. It's a delicacy that originated in the American South and we were sure we could adapt it to a kosher kitchen. After a few batches of tinkering with flavors, the chef stuck his nose into my crock pot and, with a dreamy look, said, "It smells like Texas." This was the ultimate compliment and I knew I had a winner. The recipe gets its name from the process of "pulling" or shredding the meat into slivers.

lamb shanks cassoulet

Status: Meat

Prep Time: 10 minutes

Cook Time: 6 hours

Yield: 6 servings

6 large lamb shanks

fine sea salt

freshly ground black pepper

1 (16-ounce) bag dried Northern beans, drained and rinsed

1 medium bulb fennel

3 plum tomatoes, sliced lengthwise into quarters, then sliced into ¼-inch pieces

1 Spanish onion, cut into ¼-inch dice

5 cloves fresh garlic, minced

1 tablespoon dried thyme leaves

½ tablespoon dried rosemary

½ teaspoon cracked black pepper

¼ teaspoon cayenne pepper

1 bay leaf

4 cups chicken stock

1 cup Cabernet Sauvignon or other red wine

2 cups water

6-8 ounces collard greens or kale

Line the slow cooker with a liner bag if you have one. Most require a cup or two of water in the bottom of the crock before the bag is inserted.

Season both sides of each lamb shank with salt and pepper. Stand the lamb shanks around the perimeter of the crock pot. Pour in the beans.

Remove the frond and top branches from the fennel and slice off ½ inch from the base. Discard the base. Coarsely dice the remaining fennel bulb and add it to the slow cooker. Add the sliced tomatoes and onion.

Add the garlic, thyme, rosemary, 2 teaspoons salt, ½ teaspoon cracked black pepper, cayenne pepper, bay leaf, chicken stock, wine, and water.

Break off any thick stems from the collard greens and discard. Cut the greens into small pieces; even if they are presliced in bags, slice a little more. Add them to the pot.

Roll down the liner bag. Cover the pot. Set to high and cook for 6 hours. Transfer to a serving bowl. Discard the bay leaf.

You must have a 6-quart sized crock pot for this recipe. If yours is any smaller you must halve the recipe or it won't fit. If it is just a bit smaller, like 5½ quarts, you can use a little less of the collard greens or kale.

za'atar chicken

Status: Meat

Prep Time: 5 minutes

Cook Time: 6 hours

Yield: 8 servings

8-10 chicken pieces (thighs, legs, breasts with wings removed)

1 cup dried pitted prunes

1 cup dried apricots

1 (2.5-ounce) jar green pitted Spanish olives, without pimiento, drained

1 tablespoon za'atar spice

1 teaspoon ground turmeric

1 teaspoon ground cumin

1 teaspoon onion powder

1 teaspoon garlic powder

1½ tablespoons olive oil

2 teaspoons dried oregano

Remove the skin from the chicken if desired.

Fill the bottom of slow cooker with a combination of the dried prunes and apricots in a single layer. Top with the olives.

In a small bowl, mix the za'atar spice, turmeric, cumin, onion powder, garlic powder, and olive oil. Stir to make a paste. Rub the paste all over each piece of chicken. Place the chicken on top of the olives; the parts may overlap. Sprinkle with the oregano.

Cover, and cook on low for 6 hours; do not overcook or the white meat will be very dry.

Columbus headed west across the Atlantic in search of spices and worlds were discovered. My family headed onto the streets of Jerusalem in search of chametz after Passover. Worlds were discovered here as well as we stumbled on za'atar.

That was my first trip back to Israel since becoming a foodie. I used to search for interesting Judaica. That trip I scoured Machane Yehuda for culinary treasures and discovered what Israelis think of as a common spice. They use za'atar on everything. It is a mixture of sumac, thyme, sesame seeds, oregano, marjoram, and savory.

After only a week, I had mixed it with lemon juice and olive oil to make a fabulous vinaigrette. I sprinkled it on fish and scrambled eggs. I mixed it with olive oil and brushed it on pizza dough that I baked into knots with minced garlic and oil, and I mixed some with oil into baby carrots before roasting. I am almost out and will head to the Pereg store or other good Middle Eastern source for more.

beef bourguignon

Status: Meat

Prep Time: 5 minutes

Cook Time: 4 hours

Yield: 6–8 servings

2½-3 pounds large, well-marbled beef cubes, patted dry

3 tablespoons all-purpose flour

2 tablespoons olive oil

1 (1-pound) bag frozen pearl onions, rinsed under hot water to separate, and drained

⅓ cup tomato paste

6 cloves fresh garlic, minced

1 tablespoon beef bouillon powder dissolved in 2 cups very hot water

1 cup Burgundy, Pinot Noir, or other full-bodied red wine

1 teaspoon dried rosemary, crumbled

1 teaspoon dried thyme

1 teaspoon dried parsley

¼ teaspoon fine sea salt

¼ teaspoon freshly ground black pepper

3 tablespoons Wondra flour for thickening gravy, optional

After the beef cubes have been patted dry, place them into a Ziploc bag. Add the flour and toss to coat.

Heat the oil in a very large skillet. Shake excess flour from the beef cubes and place them into the pan in a single layer, working in batches if necessary. Sear until brown on all sides, about 3 minutes per side. Remove the cubes and place them into the bowl of the slow cooker.

Add the pearl onions, tomato paste, and garlic. Stir to distribute.

Pour in the beef bouillon and wine. Sprinkle in the rosemary, thyme, parsley, salt, and pepper.

Cover the slow cooker and cook on low for 4 hours.

If you like thicker gravy, transfer the meat and onions to a serving platter. Strain the gravy into a pot. Add the Wondra flour and whisk. Bring to a simmer over medium heat, whisking until thickened. Pour the gravy over the beef.

A wonderful version of a traditional French beef stew. Serve it over a mound of mashed potatoes or rice. It is warm, filling comfort food at its best.

glazed root vegetables

Status: Parve

Prep Time: 15 minutes

Cook Time: 4½ hours

Yield: 10 servings

1 large red beet, peeled and cut into 1-inch chunks

1 large red onion, peeled and cut into 1-inch chunks

2 medium sweet potatoes, peeled and cut into 1-inch cubes

1 cup baby carrots

2 large parsnips, peeled and cut into 1-inch cubes

1 acorn squash, with skin, cut into 2-inch chunks

½ cup orange juice

3 tablespoons duck sauce

1 tablespoon coarse sea salt

¼ teaspoon dried thyme

¼ teaspoon dried rosemary, crumbled

Place the beet, onion, sweet potatoes, carrots, parsnips, and squash into the bowl of a 6-quart slow cooker. Add the orange juice, duck sauce, salt, thyme, and rosemary. Toss with a wooden spoon to combine. Cover the slow cooker and cook on high for 4½ hours.

Transfer to a serving bowl.

Don't be afraid to turn to your slow cooker for a healthful and tempting side dish. This recipe yields a bounty of gorgeous root vegetables which hit the spot on chilly fall days. The beet tinges everything a light pink. This dish will certainly please the vegetarians in your life.

SIDE DISHES

pumpkin-cranberry muffins

Status: Parve

Prep Time: 10 minutes

Cook Time: 45 minutes

Yield: 16–18 servings

3 cups bread flour or all-purpose flour

3 cups sugar

1½ teaspoons ground cinnamon

½ teaspoon baking powder

1 teaspoon baking soda

1 (15-ounce) can pumpkin (NOT pumpkin pie filling)

1 cup canola oil

3 large eggs

½ cup sweetened dried cranberries, such as Craisins

shelled pumpkin seeds

Preheat oven to 350°F. Line 3 (6-cup) muffin tins with paper muffin liners or set 16 panettone cups on a parchment-lined cookie sheet. Set aside.

In the bowl of an electric stand mixer, mix the flour, sugar, cinnamon, baking powder, and baking soda.

Add the pumpkin, oil, eggs, and cranberries. Mix on medium speed for 2 minutes.

Pour the batter into the prepared muffin tins or panettone cups. Each cup should be filled two-thirds of the way. Top each muffin with a few pumpkin seeds.

Bake, uncovered, 40–45 minutes, or until a toothpick inserted into the center of one of the muffins comes out dry. If you are using the parchment cups, which are higher, it will take a few more minutes; go by the toothpick test. Serve hot or at room temperature.

I use the taller, heavier-weight paper panettone molds instead of paper muffin cups for a more elegant look. An ice-cream scoop makes filling the cups easy and keeps everything neat.

lemon asparagus

Status: Parve

Prep Time: 5 minutes

Cook Time: 15 minutes

Yield: 6 servings

2 pounds thin asparagus, ends trimmed

2 tablespoons extra-virgin olive oil

lemon-pepper seasoning or Manischewitz Fish Seasoning

Manischewitz Creamy Horseradish Sauce with Lemon

½ lemon, optional

Preheat oven to 350°F. Line a large cookie sheet with parchment paper. Arrange the asparagus in a single layer on it.

Drizzle the olive oil over the asparagus and roll to coat. Lightly sprinkle with the seasoning.

Place, uncovered, into the oven and bake for 15 minutes, or until asparagus is bright green. Transfer to serving platter and drizzle with the Creamy Horseradish Sauce with Lemon.

Alternatively, hollow out a lemon half. Cut a thin slice from the bottom so that the lemon sits flat. Fill the lemon half with the Creamy Horseradish Sauce with Lemon. Arrange the asparagus spears in a criss-cross herringbone pattern on a large platter and place the sauce-filled lemon alongside them on the platter.

As the spokesperson for Manischewitz, I have had the pleasure of experimenting with their exciting new products. The line of Creamy Horseradish Sauces are some of my favorites, with their bold colors and great flavors. The creamy lemon horseradish sauce is a beautiful yellow hue and so simple to "make," since all you need to do is squeeze it out of the bottle!

cherry tomato crisp

Status: Parve

Prep Time: 5 minutes

Cook Time: 20 minutes

Yield: 6 servings

3 tablespoons olive oil, plus more for coating the dish

2 pints cherry tomatoes, stems removed

½ cup panko bread crumbs

2 tablespoons chopped fresh parsley

1 tablespoon dried minced onion

2 cloves fresh garlic, minced

½ teaspoon sea salt

½ teaspoon freshly ground black pepper

Preheat oven to 425°F.

Lightly coat a shallow oven-to-table baking dish with olive oil. Arrange the tomatoes in a single layer in the dish. In a medium bowl, combine the panko, parsley, minced onion, minced garlic, salt, pepper, and 3 tablespoons oil. Mix well. Sprinkle over the tomatoes.

Roast for 20–25 minutes, until crumbs are golden-brown and tomatoes are tender. Serve hot.

If you only think of crisps as being made of tree-fruit, think again! Cherry tomatoes are amazing and work great too! The stay-crisp power of panko bread crumbs make them a must for this recipe. Try not to substitute regular dried bread crumbs unless you have no choice.

sweet and sticky green beans

Status: Parve

Prep Time: 10 minutes

Cook Time: 10 minutes

Yield: 6–8 servings

2 pounds green beans, trimmed

2 tablespoons olive oil

3 large shallots, thinly sliced

3 cloves fresh garlic, thinly sliced

½ red bell pepper, cut into ¼-inch dice

½ yellow bell pepper, cut into ¼-inch dice

⅓ cup honey

3 tablespoons soy sauce

1 tablespoon cornstarch

Place the green beans into a medium pot. Cover with water. Bring to a boil over high heat and cook until the green beans turn a brighter shade, 2–3 minutes. Drain. Rinse with cold water to stop the cooking.

Meanwhile, in a large skillet, heat the olive oil over medium heat. Add the shallots and sliced garlic and cook for 2 minutes, until the garlic is fragrant but not browned. If it begins to brown, lower the heat. Add the chopped red and yellow bell peppers. Sauté for 3 minutes longer. Add the honey.

In a small bowl, dissolve the cornstarch in the soy sauce. Mix until smooth. Add to the skillet. Bring to a simmer so the sauce thickens.

Transfer the beans into the skillet. Use tongs to combine the ingredients and glaze the green beans.

A highlight of my summers is going to Camp Lavi in Pennsylvania where I spend a few days teaching teens to cook. One of the best parts is bumping into women who work there whom I knew as a kid, as well as staying up past midnight playing mah-jongg, but that's another story. Two of these friends, Hindee Rosner and Renee Levine, shared this recipe, which was making the rounds in their neighborhood. I changed it somewhat, although one of their original steps that you may want to try is tossing in ¾ cup roasted cashews at the end.

two-toned tomato pesto tart

Status: Parve

Prep Time: 10 minutes

Cook Time: 30 minutes

Yield: 9 servings

1 (17.5-ounce) box frozen puff pastry sheets, defrosted according to package directions

1 cup fresh basil leaves

1 clove fresh garlic

¼ cup pine nuts

⅓ cup extra-virgin olive oil

2 tablespoons mayonnaise

2-3 large red beefsteak tomatoes

2-3 large yellow beefsteak tomatoes

fine sea salt

freshly ground black pepper

Preheat oven to 400°F. Line a cookie sheet with parchment paper.

Place one sheet of the puff pastry on the parchment paper. Open it. Use a rolling pin to slightly flatten the sheet into a large square. Open the second puff pastry sheet. With a knife, cut 4 (1½-inch wide) long strips. Place these strips flat on top of the perimeter of the first puff pastry sheet, pulling them as necessary. This will form a puffed frame as the tart bakes and will keep the filling from leaking. With a fork, pierce the bottom of the pastry all over to allow steam to escape as the tart shell bakes. Bake the empty shell for 15 minutes.

Meanwhile, place the basil, garlic, and pine nuts into the bowl of a food processor fitted with a metal blade. Pulse until puréed. With the machine running, slowly drizzle in the olive oil and add the mayonnaise. Pulse to combine.

Remove the pastry shell from the oven. With an offset spatula, spread the pesto evenly over the inside of the pasty shell.

With a sharp serrated knife, slice the tomatoes into very thin slices. Arrange the red tomato slices in an overlapping column at one end of the tart shell. Next to it arrange the yellow tomatoes in an overlapping column. Continue in this fashion, alternating red and yellow tomato slices until the tart is covered.

Sprinkle with salt and pepper.

Return to the hot oven and bake, uncovered, for an additional 15 minutes, until pastry is puffed and golden.

For a dairy side dish, add ⅓ cup Parmesan cheese to the pesto. After cutting the strips to make the puff-pastry frame you will have some puff pastry left over. To keep it from going to waste, you can use a leaf-shaped cookie cutter to form puff–pastry leaves. Bake them on parchment alongside the tart, and place one on each serving.

braised potatoes and shallots

Status: Meat or Parve

Prep Time: 10 minutes

Cook Time: 30 minutes

Yield: 6 servings

2 tablespoons margarine

1 tablespoon olive oil

2 pounds Yukon Gold potatoes, with skin, cut into 1-inch chunks

5 medium shallots, peeled and cut into quarters

2 teaspoons dried rosemary, crumbled

1 teaspoon coarse sea salt or kosher salt

¼ teaspoon freshly ground black pepper

2 tablespoons coarse-grain or stone-ground honey-mustard, such as Honeycup brand

1 cup chicken or vegetable stock

In a large skillet over medium heat, melt the margarine. Add the olive oil and heat. Swirl to coat the sides of the pan as well as the bottom. Add the potatoes and shallots. Cook the potatoes, stirring occasionally, until browned around the edges; 8–10 minutes.

Add the rosemary, salt, and black pepper. Add the mustard and stock. Stir to distribute the mustard. Bring the stock to a boil. Cover the pan. Reduce heat to low.

Allow the potatoes to braise for about 15 minutes. The potatoes should be very tender when tested with a fork. Uncover the pan and raise the heat to medium. Use a wooden spoon to loosen the bits stuck to the pan. Reduce the liquid to a syrupy glaze. Toss to coat all the potatoes. Transfer to a serving dish. Serve hot.

Braising is a cooking method usually reserved for tough cuts of meat, but the result here is a meltingly smooth and moist potato side dish.

garlic haricots verts amandine

Status: Dairy or Parve
Prep Time: 5 minutes
Cook Time: 10 minutes
Yield: 6 servings

2 tablespoons olive oil

1 tablespoon butter or margarine

1 pound haricots verts, trimmed

5 whole garlic cloves, peeled

½ cup slivered almonds

⅛ teaspoon fine sea salt

⅛ teaspoon freshly ground black pepper

Place the oil and butter or margarine in a large skillet over medium-low heat. When it is melted, add the haricots verts. Cover and steam for 3 minutes. Uncover and stir a few times during the steaming process. Haricots verts will take a shorter time; regular green beans will take closer to 5 minutes.

Meanwhile, slice the garlic cloves into matchstick pieces, resembling the shape of the slivered almonds.

Once the green beans have turned a brighter shade of green, uncover them and add the sliced garlic. Sauté for 2–3 minutes, tossing, until garlic is fragrant but not browned.

Add the slivered almonds, salt, and pepper. Mix well; sauté for 2–3 minutes. Serve hot.

Haricots verts is the French term for "green beans." In the market, the beans carrying this name are young, long, thin, green beans. There are no strings to remove, so only the ends need trimming. In a pinch you can use regular green beans, although the haricots verts are so much more elegant-looking and have a more intense flavor.

honey-rum carrots

Status: Dairy or Parve

Prep Time: 5 minutes

Cook Time: 25 minutes

Yield: 4–6 servings

1 pound baby carrots	3 tablespoons honey
1 cup water	½ teaspoon fine sea salt
3 tablespoons butter or margarine	2 tablespoons rum or bourbon

In a skillet or pot, heat the carrots and water to boiling over high heat. Reduce the heat to low. Cover and simmer for 10 minutes, until the carrots are tender. Drain; return to the skillet.

Meanwhile, in a small saucepan, cook the butter or margarine, honey, and salt for 4–5 minutes, stirring frequently, until blended and smooth.

Add the mixture to the drained carrots. Off the heat, to avoid a flame-up, add the rum or bourbon. Cook over medium-high heat for 8–10 minutes, stirring, until carrots are tender and glazed, and the liquid has mostly evaporated.

Simple, easy, and delicious. This side dish can complement almost any main course.

sauteéd mushroom trio

Status: Parve

Prep Time: 10 minutes

Cook Time: 15 minutes

Yield: 6 servings

2 tablespoons olive oil

1 shallot, minced

6 ounces white mushrooms, cut into quarters

6 ounces shiitake mushrooms, stems removed, sliced

6 ounces crimini mushrooms, cut into quarters

½ teaspoon coarse sea salt

½ teaspoon freshly ground black pepper

3-4 sprigs fresh thyme

¼ cup Cabernet Sauvignon or other good-quality red wine

Heat the oil in a large skillet over medium heat. Add the shallot and sauté for 3–4 minutes, until shiny. Add the mushrooms and cook for 5–6 minutes, until they release their liquid.

Season with salt, pepper, and the leaves from the sprigs of thyme.

Remove the pan from the heat. Add the wine. Return to medium heat. Be careful so that the alcohol does not ignite. Cook for 3–4 minutes to cook off the alcohol. Transfer to a serving dish.

There are different schools of thought on cleaning mushrooms. I am one of those who believe that if you run them under water they will soak it up like a sponge. Instead, wipe them with a damp cloth or vegetable brush. Do not clean mushrooms until ready to use.

Kosher by Design Short on Time

SIDE DISHES

red rice

Status: Parve

Prep Time: 5 minutes

Cook Time: 1 hour

Yield: 8–10 servings

2 cups raw long-grain rice, such as Uncle Ben's Converted Original

1 (15-ounce) can tomato sauce

¼ cup ketchup

1 teaspoon fine sea salt

2 cups water

1 cup frozen mixed vegetables (peas, carrots, green beans, and corn)

Preheat oven to 350°F.

Pour the rice into an 9- by 13-inch or large oval oven-to-table baking dish.

Add the tomato sauce, ketchup, salt, and water. Stir to combine. Stir in the frozen vegetables. Cover tightly with foil.

Bake for 1 hour. Remove the foil; allow to stand at room temperature for 5 minutes. Scrape a fork over the grains in all directions to fluff rice and distribute the sauce.

This is a dish linked to happy childhood memories from time spent in the home of my lifelong friend Shari Wiesel. Her mom Betty would throw this recipe together for almost every Shabbos without any measurements or written notes. The smells from my experimentation took me right back to the yellow walls and cozy round kitchen nook where we shared so many meals and as many games of Rummy-O. This side dish was always my favorite and now that I have been able to put together a written recipe, I know it will be a favorite of your kids as well.

orange cornmeal bread

Status: Dairy or Parve

Prep Time: 10 minutes

Cook Time: 30 minutes

Yield: 9 servings

1 cup all-purpose flour

1 cup yellow cornmeal

¾ cup sugar

2 teaspoons baking powder

1 teaspoon fine sea salt

¼ teaspoon baking soda

2 large eggs

1 navel orange

1 cup buttermilk or soy milk

1 tablespoon lemon juice, optional for parve version only

4 tablespoons butter or margarine, melted

Preheat oven to 400°F. Heavily grease and flour an 8- by 8-inch square pan. For ease, you can use the spray that has oil and flour in the can. Set aside.

In a medium bowl, whisk the flour, cornmeal, sugar, baking powder, salt, and baking soda.

In another bowl, whisk together the eggs and juice of the orange. If preparing the dairy version, add the buttermilk. If parve, measure 1 cup soy milk and remove 1 tablespoon. Add the lemon juice to the soy milk. Mix and add to the eggs. Whisk in the melted butter or margarine.

Add the egg mixture to the dry ingredients, using a wooden spoon to combine.

Spoon into the prepared pan. Bake, uncovered, for 27–30 minutes or until lightly browned and a toothpick inserted in center comes out dry. Cool and slice.

The juice from the orange takes care of the age-old problem of bone-dry cornbread. It also adds a brightness that makes this a lovely side dish. This recipe can serve double duty as a great addition to a brunch table; serve slices spread with very soft butter.

creamy french-fried vegetables

Status: Parve

Prep Time: 5 minutes

Cook Time: 35 minutes

Yield: 6–8 servings

2 (1-pound) bags frozen California-mix vegetables (carrots, broccoli, cauliflower)

2 (14.5-ounce) cans cream-style corn

2 (2.8-ounce) cans french-fried onions, such as French's

Preheat oven to 350°F.

Place the frozen mixed vegetables into a strainer. Run them under warm water to separate them and melt any ice crystals. Drain very well.

Place the vegetables into a medium oven-to-table casserole or divide them into 6 (6-ounce) ramekins for individual portions.

Top the vegetables with the cream-style corn. Sprinkle on the fried onions.

Cover the casserole or ramekins with foil and bake for 30 minutes. Uncover and bake until the onions are crispy, about 5–6 minutes. Serve hot.

My mom used to make this as a last-minute side dish when I was a kid. The fried onions have gone in and out of parve certification and so the recipe went in and out of my repertoire. Happily, they are parve again and my family is back in business! If you are going to reheat this dish, make sure it is uncovered or else the onion rings will get mushy.

sesame spinach sushi

Status: Parve

Prep Time: 10 minutes

Cook Time: 5 minutes

Yield: 6 servings

4 (9-ounce) bags fresh spinach leaves

½ cup sesame seeds

2 tablespoons soy sauce

2 tablespoons roasted or toasted sesame oil

2 tablespoons sugar

Pour ½-inch water into a large pot. Add the spinach. Bring the heat to medium and cover the pot. Cook the spinach for 2–3 minutes, or until hot and just wilted. Drain the water, pressing out as much as possible. Return the spinach to the pot.

Meanwhile, in a small frying pan, spread the sesame seeds in a single layer and heat them over medium heat for 30–60 seconds, or until they turn golden-brown or start to pop. Remove from heat.

In a small bowl, mix the soy sauce, sesame oil, and sugar until the sugar dissolves.

Add this soy-sauce mixture to the spinach.

Divide the spinach into thirds and place each onto a piece of parchment paper or a sushi mat. Roll it, using the paper to help form it into a skinny log. Open the paper. Cut each log into slices about 1-inch thick and dip one end of each slice into the toasted sesame seeds.

Place on a platter. Serve with pan juices or soy sauce.

This dish is healthy and delicious. It is also easy to make; just start with the pre-washed bags of spinach leaves. You would not believe how little 36 ounces of spinach cooks down into!

When you are really short on time, there is no need to roll the spinach. Just toss it with the toasted sesame seeds and serve in a pretty serving dish.

spicy potato stacks

Status: Parve

Prep Time: 10 minutes

Cook Time: 20 minutes

Yield: 6–8 potato stacks

2 large Yukon Gold potatoes, unpeeled, sliced into ½-inch slices, ends discarded

2 large red potatoes, unpeeled, sliced into ½-inch slices, ends discarded

2 sweet potatoes, peeled, sliced into ½-inch slices, ends discarded

½ cup extra-virgin olive oil

2 tablespoons barbecue spice blend (try to find one with hickory flavor)

fresh rosemary sprigs

fine sea salt

Preheat oven to 400°F. Cover a large jelly roll pan or cookie sheet with parchment paper. Set aside.

Place all the sliced potatoes into a large mixing bowl.

Pour the oil into the bowl. Toss to coat. Sprinkle in the spice blend. Toss to coat well. Arrange the potatoes in a single layer on prepared baking sheet. Roast the potatoes, uncovered, for 20 minutes.

Season with a sprinkle of salt.

Make layered stacks using the three kinds of potatoes. Stick a rosemary skewer through the top to secure each stack. Serve hot.

Look for potatoes of similar diameter so that they line up easily when stacked. You should be able to get 3 to 4 slices from the Yukon Gold and red potatoes and 5 to 6 slices from each sweet potato. To make these stacks hot and spicy, add cayenne pepper to the barbecue spice blend. You can also slice an onion into very thin rings, coat with the same spices and roast alongside the potatoes. Insert a roasted onion slice between each potato slice.

cauliflower française

Status: Meat or Parve

Prep Time: 10 minutes

Cook Time: 25 minutes

Yield: 6–8 servings

2 heads cauliflower

1 cup plus 1½ tablespoons all-purpose flour, divided

fine sea salt

freshly ground black pepper

3 large eggs

olive-oil-flavored cooking spray

3 tablespoons margarine, divided

juice of 1 lemon

1 cup white wine

½ cup chicken or vegetable stock

3 tablespoons chopped fresh curly parsley

Preheat the oven to 425°F. Cover 2 large cookie sheets with parchment paper. Set aside.

Trim the cauliflower to the base so that it sits flat on the cutting board. Trim off the two outer ends. Make 3 (¾-inch) lengthwise cuts to yield 3–4 large steaks from each head of cauliflower. Keep the remaining pieces that fall off as flat intact bunches as much as possible.

In a shallow bowl or pie plate, stir together the 1 cup flour, ½ teaspoon salt, and ¼ teaspoon pepper. Dredge the large cauliflower steaks, one at a time, in the flour mixture, shaking off the excess. Toss the smaller pieces in the flour and shake off excess. Lightly beat eggs in another shallow bowl or pie plate. Dip the floured cauliflower into the eggs to coat, letting the excess drip off; then place in single layers on prepared cookie sheets.

Once all the cauliflower is battered, spray the tops of the cauliflower steaks and pieces with olive-oil-flavored cooking spray. Season with salt and pepper. Place into the hot oven and bake for 20–25 minutes or until the cauliflower is tender.

In a medium skillet, melt the margarine. Whisk in the 1½ tablespoons flour. Add the juice of the lemon, wine, and stock. Season with ¼ teaspoon salt and ¼ teaspoon pepper. Bring to a simmer and cook for 4 minutes. Stir in the parsley. Taste and re-season as needed. Spoon sauce over the cauliflower.

Française is generally a preparation reserved for chicken or thinly sliced veal. I thought I would try it with cauliflower, one of my favorite vegetables. The results? C'est magnifique!

corn flake-topped carrot kugel

Status: Parve
Prep Time: 10 minutes
Cook Time: 1 hour
Yield: 9 servings

4 (4-ounce) jars baby-food carrots
¾ cups (1½ sticks) margarine, divided
1 cup sugar
1 cup all-purpose flour
3 large eggs

¼ cup soy milk
¼ cup brown sugar
2 cups corn flakes, whole (do not crush)

Preheat oven to 350°F. Spray a 9-inch round or square baking pan with nonstick cooking spray. Set aside.

Melt ½ cup (1 stick) margarine in a small saucepan or in the microwave.

In the bowl of a stand mixer, beat the baby-food carrots, melted margarine, sugar, flour, eggs, and soy milk until smooth; pour into the prepared pan.

In a medium pot, over medium heat, melt the brown sugar with the 4 remaining tablespoons margarine. When the mixture is melted and smooth, remove from heat and mix in the corn flakes. With a wooden spoon, toss to coat all the flakes; try to keep them whole.

Sprinkle the corn flakes evenly over the top of the kugel; do not mix in.

Bake, uncovered, for 1 hour. Serve warm.

A smooth, dense kugel with a crown of golden caramelized crunch. Yum, yum, and yum. Nothing more to say.

thai quinoa

Status: Parve

Prep Time: 10 minutes

Cook Time: 15 minutes

Yield: 6–8 servings

1½ cups dry quinoa

3 cups water

1 jalapeño pepper, seeded and minced

6 leaves fresh basil, finely chopped

3 sprigs fresh cilantro, leaves gently torn (discard stems)

⅓ cup minced red onion (about ½ small red onion)

½ firm mango, not too ripe, peeled, pitted, and cut into ⅛-inch dice

2 tablespoons extra-virgin olive oil

1 tablespoon soy sauce

fine sea salt

1 tablespoon lime juice

Rinse the quinoa thoroughly either in a strainer or in a pot and drain. (Do not skip this step or a bitter-tasting, natural soap-like coating will remain.) Once the quinoa is drained, place it into a medium pot with the water. Bring to a boil. Reduce the heat and simmer until the water is absorbed, about 10–15 minutes or until the grains turn translucent and the outer layer pops off. Drain.

Meanwhile, in a medium bowl, combine the minced jalapeño, basil, cilantro, red onion, and mango. Drizzle in the oil, soy sauce, ½ teaspoon salt, and lime juice. Stir to combine.

Add the drained quinoa and toss to combine. Season with salt to taste. Serve warm or at room temperature.

Quinoa has become very popular with cooks today, especially during Passover when this berry, which tastes like a grain, stands in nicely for what we crave. It is high in protein and has other healthful characteristics. Quinoa is small, like couscous or millet, and can be seasoned in endless ways.

tzimmes puffs

Status: Parve

Prep Time: 10 minutes

Cook Time: 25 minutes

Yield: 18 puffs

18 puff pastry squares or 1 (17.5-ounce) box frozen puff pastry sheets, defrosted according to package directions

1½ cups firmly packed sweet potatoes, from a 28-ounce can, drained

1 cup frozen carrot coins or frozen baby carrots

¼ cup whole berry cranberry sauce

1 (8-ounce) can crushed pineapple, drained

2 tablespoons all-purpose flour

2 tablespoons dark-brown sugar

Preheat oven to 400°F. Spray muffin tins with nonstick cooking spray. Set aside.

Lay out the puff pastry squares on a work surface or cut each puff pastry sheet into 9 equal squares to total 18 squares.

Empty the drained sweet potatoes into a medium bowl. Mash with the back of a fork. Combine with the carrots, cranberry sauce, crushed pineapple, flour, and brown sugar. Toss to combine.

Place a heaping tablespoon of filling into the center of each pastry square.

Moisten the edges of each square with water. Gently stretch the dough and pull the two sets of opposite corners so they almost meet in the center, leaving some of the filling visible. Let all four triangular tips flop over; they will open slightly as they bake.

Place each puff pastry packet into the cup of a muffin tin.

Bake, uncovered for 20–25 minutes, until puffed and golden. Serve warm.

My mom and I are big tzimmes fans. Over the years we have tasted many versions. Some have brisket; others have prunes; all are sweet and delicious.

This quick and easy dish takes some of the main ingredients in tzimmes and wraps them up in what I consider the Pepperidge Farm company's gift to the Jews, parve puff pastry. Could there be anything more fabulous?

roasted-garlic asparagus

Status: Parve
Prep Time: 5 minutes
Cook Time: 15 minutes
Yield: 6 servings

½ cup extra-virgin olive oil

8 cloves fresh garlic, minced

1 teaspoon onion powder

2 tablespoons fresh finely chopped parsley

2 pounds thin asparagus, ends trimmed

coarse sea salt or fleur de sel

freshly ground black pepper

Preheat oven to 400°F. Line a large jelly-roll pan with parchment paper. Set aside.

In a small pot, over medium-low, heat the oil, garlic, onion powder, and parsley. Cook for 3 minutes, until the garlic mixture is fragrant but not browned.

Spread the asparagus in a single layer on the prepared sheet. Lightly sprinkle with coarse sea salt and freshly ground pepper. Drizzle on the garlic-oil mixture.

Roast for 8–10 minutes, until the asparagus is bright green; do not overcook.

Transfer to a platter and serve hot.

Simple, elegant, healthy. What more could you want from a side dish? For a prettier presentation, you can trim the "thorns" from the asparagus with a vegetable peeler.

DESSERTS

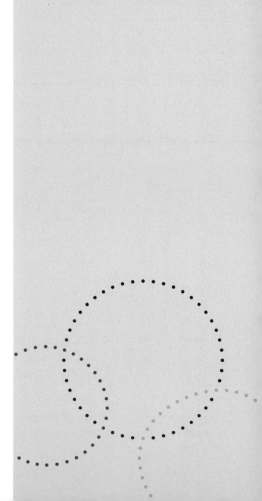

brownie bites

Status: Parve

Prep Time: 10 minutes

Cook Time: 40 minutes

Yield: 36 brownie bites

½ cup (1 stick) unsalted margarine, melted and placed in refrigerator to cool for 10 minutes

¾ cup good-quality Dutch process cocoa powder, such as Droste brand

¼ cup vegetable or canola oil

2 cups sugar

1 cup all-purpose flour

3 large eggs

1 teaspoon pure vanilla extract

COATING:

confectioner's sugar

cocoa powder

chopped nuts

edible glitter

colored sanding sugars

Preheat oven to 325°F. Line a 7- by 11-inch brownie pan with parchment paper and coat with nonstick cooking spray.

In the bowl of an electric stand mixer, combine the melted margarine, cocoa powder, oil, sugar, flour, eggs, and vanilla. Beat to combine.

Spread the mixture into the prepared pan.

Bake for 35–40 minutes. Remove the pan from the oven and place into the refrigerator to cool for 20 minutes or until cool enough to handle.

When the brownies are cool, run a knife around the edge of the pan. Flip the brownie out onto a piece of parchment paper on a hard work surface in one whole piece. Using a 1½-inch diameter round cookie cutter, cut circles from the center of the brownie, leaving the harder crust. Roll the circles between the palms of your hands to form into balls, and roll into coating of your choice.

Store in an airtight container.

Although a good brownie never gets boring, sometimes I like a dessert that may be just as easy but is visually more exciting. There is something elegant and grown-up about this recipe, and how it's presented, but the rich chocolaty brownie flavor will still appeal to kids.

Or, I'll just come clean and admit that I love making this because my favorite part of any brownie is the very edge, the harder, chewier part. This recipe leaves that over, or I should say, leaves that all for me!

berry swirl cheesecake triangles

Status: Dairy

Prep Time: 10 minutes

Cook Time: 1 hour

Yield: 12 servings

CRUST:

1¾ cups all-purpose flour

½ cup confectioner's sugar

½ teaspoon fine sea salt

1 cup (2 sticks) unsalted butter, cold, cut into small pieces

1 tablespoon ice water

FILLING:

2 (8-ounce) blocks cream cheese, at room temperature for 15 minutes

½ cup sugar

1 teaspoon pure vanilla extract

2 large eggs

½ cup good-quality blueberry preserves

½ cup good-quality seedless raspberry or strawberry preserves

Preheat oven to 350°F. Line 9- by 13-inch baking pan with parchment paper or heavily grease the pan with butter. Set aside.

In the bowl of an electric stand mixer, mix the flour, confectioner's sugar, and salt. Using a low speed to prevent the flour from spilling, add in the bits of butter and mix until dough begins to form. Add the ice water to make a smooth dough. This can also be done in a food processor.

Press the dough evenly into the prepared pan. Bake for 20 minutes or until the crust is lightly golden.

While the crust is cooling, prepare the filling: In the bowl of an electric stand mixer, beat the cream cheese with the sugar, vanilla, and eggs on medium speed until the batter is smooth. Pour it over the prepared crust.

Dollop the blueberry preserves randomly over the batter. Dollop the raspberry preserves between these dollops of blueberry. Use a knife to swirl and combine the berries and batter. Bake for 40 minutes or until the center is set.

Cool completely. Cut into 6 squares, then cut each square diagonally in half to make triangles. Store, covered, in the refrigerator.

Each summer my parents babysit and my husband and I are treated to a getaway. We usually pick someplace that is a short flight, has a minor league baseball team (no, that is not MY criteria,) and some Jewish interest. Last summer we vacationed in Portland, Maine, a most relaxing and beautiful place. In the quaint shopping district, recipe cards for a version of this dessert were being given out in the Stonewall Kitchen store.

Their samples looked dreamy so when I came home I whipped up a batch. I am a huge fan of cheesecake in all of its incarnations. This creamy version over a cookie crust is no exception. I added my own twist and ideas to their basic recipe. The berries here add a great visual and taste effect and the cooking time is shorter than that of a traditional cheesecake.

peanut butter mousse

Status: Dairy or Parve

Prep Time: 10 minutes

Cook Time: none

Needs chill time

Yield: 8 servings

1 (8-ounce) block cream cheese or nondairy cream cheese such as Tofutti brand

1 cup creamy peanut butter

1 tablespoon pure vanilla extract

1 cup confectioner's sugar, sifted

1 cup heavy cream or nondairy whipping cream (for parve I like Richwhip brand)

6 ounces chocolate chips, optional for garnish

1 tablespoon corn syrup or vegetable shortening such as Crisco, optional for garnish

In the bowl of an electric stand mixer, beat the cream cheese, peanut butter, and vanilla extract on medium speed until smooth. Add the confectioner's sugar and beat on high speed until well-incorporated.

When the mixture is combined and smooth, pour in the cream. Mix on low speed and then beat on high for 4 minutes.

Pour into serving dish. Refrigerate for 20 minutes or more until firm.

If making the garnish, melt the chocolate with the corn syrup or shortening in a small container in the microwave, on medium power for 2–3 minutes. Stir at 30-second intervals. Scoop into a heavy-duty quart-sized Ziploc bag. Snip the corner. Line a cookie sheet with parchment paper. Drizzle chocolate onto the prepared sheet, making zigzags in both directions to form 8 lattices. Place into the refrigerator to chill and firm.

Place a lattice on each dessert plate and top each with a scoop of Peanut Butter Mousse.

This mousse recipe is so creamy, it is perfect alone or garnished with a chocolate lattice.

When I am not short on time, the recipe is part of a signature dessert of mine. I serve a scoop of this mousse with a scoop of chocolate mousse and garnish the dish with a Peanut Butter cookie (recipe in Kosher by Design — Kids in the Kitchen, page 182) and a Double Chocolate Cookie (recipe in Kosher by Design Entertains, page 289). It is a show-stopper!

lemon mousse parfaits

Status: Dairy or Parve

Prep Time: 10 minutes

Cook Time: 5 minutes

Needs chill time

Yield: 6 servings

¾ cup sugar

1 tablespoon cornstarch

2 large eggs

3 large egg yolks

zest of 2 lemons (yellow part only, not the white pith)

juice of 3 lemons

1 cup heavy cream or nondairy whipping cream (for parve I like Richwhip brand)

½ cup confectioner's sugar

blueberries or raspberries

Combine the sugar and cornstarch in a heavy medium-sized pot. Whisk in the eggs, egg yolks, lemon zest, and lemon juice until blended.

Place a strainer over a medium bowl. Set aside.

Turn the heat to medium and cook the mixture, whisking continuously, until it is thick and bubbly, about 3–4 minutes. Whisk for 1 minute longer. Remove from the heat.

Pour the lemon mixture through the strainer set over the medium bowl, using your whisk to push it through. The zest and egg solids will get caught in the strainer and should be discarded.

Lay a sheet of plastic wrap directly on the lemon curd, touching the surface so that it does not form a skin. Place in the freezer to quickly cool while you whip the cream.

In the bowl of an electric stand mixer, beat the cream on high speed until it is thick and stiff peaks form. Slowly beat in the confectioner's sugar until it is all incorporated.

Remove the lemon curd from the freezer. Using a spatula, fold in one-third of the whipped cream to lighten the mixture. Fold in remaining cream until it is an even pale-yellow color. Refrigerate until needed.

Put a handful of blueberries or raspberries into each of 6 wine glasses or other stemmed glasses. Top with lemon mousse. Serve chilled.

For a light, ethereal ending to a meal, try this lemon mousse. The lemon color and flavor are both complemented by the fresh berries. In this recipe, homemade lemon curd is transformed into mousse with whipped cream.

giant zebra fudge cookies

Status: Parve

Prep Time: 5 minutes

Cook Time: 18 minutes

Yield: 18 large cookies

½ cup canola or vegetable oil

2 cups sugar

2 cups all-purpose flour

1 cup good-quality Dutch process cocoa powder, such as Droste brand

4 large eggs

1 teaspoon pure vanilla extract

2 teaspoons baking powder

confectioner's sugar

Preheat oven to 350°F. Line 2 large cookie sheets or jelly-roll pans with parchment paper. Set aside.

In the bowl of an electric stand mixer, mix the oil, sugar, flour, cocoa powder, eggs, vanilla, and baking powder, until a soft dough forms

Roll the dough into 18 balls slightly larger than golf balls.

Fill a small bowl with confectioner's sugar and stir with a fork to break up any clumps. Lower the balls, one at a time, into the bowl of confectioner's sugar and toss to coat heavily and completely. Transfer to prepared pans. Leave room between the dough balls, as the cookies spread during baking.

Bake for 18 minutes. If you like, you can make smaller cookies; form walnut-sized balls and bake for 12 minutes.

Cool completely.

I do many cooking demonstrations all over the country and each one is wonderful and memorable. One last year was for Kimpitorin Aid, which helps new mothers. The hostess, Goldie Stern, set the event in a tent decorated with lights, white paper balls from the ceiling, vines, trees, and berries. She coordinated the look down to pieces of tree trunk to hold the platters. So there I was in this gorgeous environment, prepared to cook and teach about fabulous food, MY fabulous food, and all I heard were murmuring about an awesome cookie that Goldie's sister-in-law, Zipporah Farkas, had made for the event.

Guests kept gravitating over to the cookie table, whispering to their neighbors about these cookies. Well, I have to say, I had never been upstaged by a cookie before, but it clearly happened that night. I felt that the only appropriate payback was for Zipporah to give me the recipe to use in this book. She was adorable and obliged. She credits it to her friend Rivki Shaulson. I guess if I have to share the spotlight with a cookie, I'm glad it is such a pretty, yummy, fudgy one.

cookie brittle

Status: Dairy or Parve

Prep Time: 5 minutes

Cook Time: 25 minutes

Yield: 20–25 servings

1 cup (2 sticks) unsalted butter or margarine, at room temperature

1 cup sugar

1½ teaspoons pure vanilla extract

1 teaspoon fine sea salt

2 cups all-purpose flour

10 ounces good-quality semi-sweet chocolate chips

Preheat the oven to 350°F. Line a 10- by 15-inch jelly roll pan with parchment paper.

With an electric stand mixer, cream the butter or margarine with the sugar on medium speed until light yellow and smooth. Add the vanilla and salt.

Slowly add the flour and mix until incorporated. Stir in the chocolate chips.

Press the dough into a thin, even layer in the prepared pan. I like to cover the dough with a sheet of parchment paper and use a small rolling pin or a heavy can to quickly and evenly spread the dough.

Bake 20–25 minutes or until golden-brown.

Cool completely. Break into pieces with your hands to create uneven shards of cookie brittle.

This quick and easy recipe came from my friend Karen Zomick Finkelstein. Zomick is the key word here, as she comes from a famous name in kosher bakeries. This recipe is a great way to get a large batch of cookies on the table very quickly.

strawberry streusel cake

Status: Dairy or Parve

Prep Time: 10 minutes

Cook Time: 45 minutes

Yield: 8 servings

2 cups all-purpose flour

½ cup sugar

½ teaspoon fine sea salt

1 tablespoon baking powder

1 teaspoon ground cinnamon

2 large eggs

1 cup milk or soy milk

⅓ cup canola or vegetable oil

1 teaspoon pure vanilla extract

1 (10-ounce) jar thick strawberry jam or preserves

STREUSEL CRUMB TOPPING:

¾ cup all-purpose flour

½ cup sugar

1 tablespoon ground cinnamon

1 teaspoon pure vanilla extract

6 tablespoons (¾ stick) unsalted butter or margarine, melted

Preheat oven to 375°F. Spray a 9½-inch springform pan with nonstick cooking spray. Set aside.

In the bowl of an electric stand mixer, combine the flour, sugar, salt, baking powder, and cinnamon. Add the eggs and beat on medium speed. Add the milk, oil, and vanilla. Beat until the mixture is smooth.

Pour the batter into the prepared pan. Spoon the strawberry jam over the batter. Use a knife or spatula to make shallow swirls to ripple the jam into the cake batter.

Make the streusel crumb topping: In a medium bowl, use your fingertips to pinch the flour, sugar, cinnamon, vanilla, and melted butter or margarine into coarse crumbs. Sprinkle the streusel crumbs all over the top of the cake.

Bake, uncovered for 45 minutes, or until a toothpick inserted into the center comes out clean. Allow the cake to cool for a few minutes. Release the sides of the pan. Cool completely and slice.

Every spring when the weather turns warm, my husband and I take our kids to the farms in Princeton, NJ to pick strawberries. It is the sure sign that summer is just around the corner. We always make sure to pick extra pints, at least one to share on the drive home from the farm, and at least two to bring home to dip into chocolate.

In the winter, when strawberries are out of season, I whip up this cake. With its hint of strawberry and cozy coffee-cake feel, it is perfect with a cup of coffee or tea and it brings me back to picking berries with my family under the warm sun.

Feel free to substitute other flavors of preserves.

lemon drops

Status: Dairy or Parve

Prep Time: 10 minutes

Cook Time: 12 minutes

Yield: 22–25 lemon drops

½ cup (1 stick) unsalted butter or margarine, softened at room temperature for 10 minutes

½ cup plus 1 tablespoon sugar or superfine sugar

1 large egg yolk

½ teaspoon pure vanilla extract

½ teaspoon pure lemon extract

1½ cups all-purpose flour

¼ teaspoon salt

1 tablespoon milk or vanilla soy milk

1 cup confectioner's sugar

1 can lemon pie filling or 1 jar lemon curd, such as Dickenson's brand

Preheat oven to 375°F. Line 2 large cookie sheets with parchment paper. Set aside.

In the bowl of an electric stand mixer, beat the butter or margarine and the sugar on high speed, until smooth and creamy. Add the egg yolk and vanilla and lemon extracts. Mix for 1 minute, scraping down the sides.

In a medium bowl, sift the flour and salt together. Add half the flour mixture to the egg mixture. Add the milk and then the remaining flour mixture. Mix until just combined. Set aside.

Place the dough between two pieces of parchment paper and, with a rolling pin, flatten to ¼-inch thickness. Using the top of a spice jar (see note), or a 1½-inch round cookie cutter, cut out cookies. Re-roll the scraps into another mound of dough to be rolled out.

Place the rounds 1½-inches apart on the prepared cookie sheets. Bake for 10–12 minutes or until golden. Remove from oven and let cool for 10 minutes.

Fill a fine mesh sieve with the confectioner's sugar. Hold it over the cookies and tap the sieve lightly with a fork or spoon to shake out the sugar, completely covering the cookies.

When the cookies are completely cool, turn 1 cookie over, spread a small dollop of lemon pie filling on each and top with a second cookie to form a sandwich. Repeat with remaining cookies until all cookies are used up.

This is a beautiful cookie. The dough is so simple to make and work with, plus there is no waiting for dough to chill. In place of a round cookie cutter, I use the lid of my 1-ounce McCormick cinnamon spice jar or any spice jar. Just wash it out so it does not smell like the spice. It is the perfect size, and gives the cookie just the right mounded shape and diameter.

If you like your cookies crunchy, don't fill until ready to serve. If you like softer cookies, fill them in advance. Lemon curd is usually dairy, so go with the pie filling for the parve version or for a little sweeter touch.

cookies and cream pots de crème

Status: Dairy or Parve

Prep Time: 5 minutes

Cook Time: none

Needs chill time

Yield: 6 (4-ounce) servings

6 large egg yolks

1 teaspoon pure vanilla extract

¼ teaspoon salt

2 cups (12-ounces) good-quality semi-sweet chocolate chips

1½ cups light cream or vanilla soy milk

6 Oreo cookies or parve chocolate sandwich cookies

1 cup heavy cream or nondairy whipping cream (for parve I like Richwhip brand)

3 tablespoons confectioner's sugar

In a small bowl or cup, place the egg yolks, vanilla, and salt. Set aside.

Place the chocolate chips into the bowl of a food processor fitted with a metal blade, or in a blender. Process the chocolate chips for 1 minute.

Meanwhile, heat the cream or soy milk in a small pot over medium heat. When it just begins to boil, pour it over the chocolate in the food processor. Cover and pulse for 30 seconds to melt the chocolate.

Add the egg-yolk mixture. Pulse for 10 seconds, until smooth.

Pour into 6 teacups or pots de crème bowls.

Break 1 cookie into each cup. Gently stir.

Place the pots de crème into the refrigerator to chill for 3–4 hours.

Beat the heavy or nondairy whipping cream with the confectioner's sugar in a mixer on high speed until soft peaks form.

Serve the pots de crème with whipped cream.

This speedy recipe gives me the chance to break out my grandmother's gorgeous antique teacups. Feel free to experiment with other flavors; try adding some mint extract or rum in place of the vanilla, or leave out the cookies for plain pots de crème.

frosted honey-chocolate cake

Status: Dairy or Parve
Prep Time: 10 minutes
Cook Time: 45 minutes
Yield: 9 servings

3 ounces good-quality semi-sweet chocolate bar, such as Noblesse

⅔ cup honey

1½ cups all-purpose flour

1 teaspoon baking soda

¾ teaspoon salt

½ cup (1 stick) unsalted butter or margarine

½ cup sugar

1 teaspoon pure vanilla extract

2 large eggs

⅔ cup milk or soy milk

HONEY FROSTING:

8 ounces cream cheese or parve cream cheese, such as Tofutti brand, not whipped

½ cup (1 stick) unsalted butter or margarine, at room temperature

¼ cup honey

Preheat oven to 350°F. Grease a 9-inch square baking pan with nonstick cooking spray and line it with parchment paper, or grease and flour the pan. The cake will turn out onto a serving plate more easily when you use the parchment paper. Set aside.

Break the chocolate up and place into a microwave-safe dish with the honey. Microwave for 45–60 seconds. Stir after 20 seconds to hasten the melting.

Place the flour, baking soda, and salt in a medium bowl. Whisk to combine. Set aside.

In the bowl of a stand mixer, beat the butter or margarine with the sugar on high speed until creamy. Add the vanilla, eggs, and the chocolate-honey mixture.

Add half the flour mixture with half the milk. Mix. Add the remaining flour mixture and remaining milk. Beat until smooth.

Pour into the prepared pan. Bake for 35–40 minutes, or until a toothpick inserted into the center comes out clean. After cooling for 10 minutes, run a thin metal spatula around the edges and turn the cake out onto a cooling rack or cake plate.

While cake is cooling, prepare the frosting: Place the cream cheese in the microwave and heat for 2 (15-second) intervals to soften. Stir.

In the bowl of a stand mixer, beat the butter or margarine and cream cheese until smooth. With the beater going, drizzle in the honey. Beat until just mixed and creamy. Do not over-beat or the honey will separate. Spread the frosting over the top of the cooled cake. If making the frosting in advance, store in the refrigerator.

Here is a twist for Rosh Hashana, when many people serve traditional honey cake. The honey frosting is divine. It is reminiscent of a good cream cheese frosting from carrot cake.

funnel cakes

Status: Dairy or Parve

Prep Time: 10 minutes

Cook Time: 10 minutes

Yield: 10 funnel cakes

canola or vegetable oil

2½ cups all-purpose flour

½ cup sugar

2 tablespoons baking powder

1 teaspoon salt

1 cup milk or soy milk

1 cup water, plus more as needed

1 teaspoon pure vanilla extract

1 large egg

confectioner's sugar, for dusting

In a 10-inch skillet, heat ¾-inch of oil over medium heat, to 375°F.

Meanwhile, in a medium bowl, combine the flour, sugar, baking powder, and salt. Set aside.

In the bowl of a mixer, beat the milk, 1 cup water, vanilla, and egg on medium-high speed. Add the dry ingredients and beat until smooth.

Hold a thumb over the bottom opening of a funnel. Using a ladle or measuring cup, pour batter into the funnel. Release your thumb and drop the batter into the oil in a circular and zigzag motion. Do not fill entire skillet since the batter expands and puffs as it cooks. If the batter is too thick to run through the funnel, add water, a tablespoon at a time, up to maximum of 7 or 8 tablespoons, to thin it.

Fry for 30 seconds or until the edges are golden-brown. Using tongs, turn the funnel cake over and fry 20 seconds longer. Remove the funnel cake to paper towels to drain. Dust with confectioner's sugar. Repeat with remaining batter.

These are right out of a carnival or street fair. My kids love them, but I think I love them even more. At the photo shoot for this book, the food stylist spelled my name out in funnel cakes, the best reward for a long day's work!

It takes a little practice to get them right, but once you do, you will be popping these out in no time. The key to success is in the temperature of the oil. Too cool and the funnel cakes will be greasy. Too hot and they will burn. The oil must be 375°F, and a thermometer is the only way to judge that. Pyrex makes a good, small, inexpensive digital thermometer that goes up to 400°F. You can also use a candy thermometer.

This same recipe makes great apple fritters. Peel, core, and slice three apples into ¼-inch rings. Lightly coat in flour, shaking off excess. Prepare batter as directed. Dip the apple rings into the batter, shake off excess, and fry. Sprinkle with confectioner's sugar and cinnamon.

black-cherry crumble bars

Status: Dairy or Parve
Prep Time: 10 minutes
Cook Time: 40 minutes
Yield: 20 bars

1 ½ cups all-purpose flour

½ cup sugar

1 ½ teaspoons baking powder

¼ teaspoon fine sea salt

¼ cup (½ stick) unsalted butter or margarine, melted

CRUMB TOPPING:

¾ cup all-purpose flour

½ cup light-brown sugar

½ teaspoon ground cinnamon

1 large egg, slightly beaten

3 tablespoons light cream or soy milk

1 teaspoon pure vanilla extract

1 (12-14 ounce) jar good-quality black-cherry or other preserves, such as Hero or Sarabeth's brands

¼ cup (½-stick) unsalted butter or margarine, melted

Preheat oven to 350°F. Spray a 9- by 13-inch metal baking pan with nonstick cooking spray. Line the pan with parchment paper, allowing some overhang so you can easily remove and cut the bars after baking.

In the bowl of an electric stand mixer, mix the flour, sugar, baking powder, and salt on medium speed to combine.

Add melted butter or margarine, egg, cream or soy milk, and vanilla. Mix on medium speed until a smooth dough forms. Pat the dough into the prepared pan.

With a thin metal spatula, spread the black-cherry preserves evenly over the top of the dough.

Prepare the crumb topping: In a small bowl, combine the flour, brown sugar, cinnamon, and melted butter or margarine. Use your fingers to pinch into coarse crumbs.

Sprinkle the crumbs over the top of the black-cherry filling.

Bake for 35–40 minutes, until the crumbs are a medium-brown color.

Cool for 5–10 minutes. Using the parchment paper, remove from the pan in one sheet; cut into squares.

These crumble bars are a great pantry item when you need to whip up a dessert without running out to the market. You can use whatever flavor good-quality preserves you have in your house. I have tried blueberry, strawberry, and apricot, but the black-cherry bars are my favorite.

caramel nut bars

Status: Dairy or Parve

Prep Time: 15 minutes

Cook Time: 20 minutes

Needs chill time

Yield: 48 bars

CRUST:

½ cup (1 stick) unsalted butter or margarine, at room temperature, cut into small pieces

½ cup light-brown sugar

1 ¼ cups all-purpose flour

½ teaspoon salt

CARAMEL NUT LAYER:

1 batch Thick Caramel (see page 304)

½ cup salted cocktail peanuts

½ cup salted cashews

Prepare a batch of Thick Caramel as directed. While it is cooling, prepare the crust.

Preheat oven to 350°F. Lightly grease a 9- by 13-inch baking pan with nonstick cooking spray. Line it with parchment paper, allowing the paper to come up over the sides. Set aside.

In the bowl of an electric stand mixer, mix the margarine and brown sugar at medium/high speed until creamy. Add the flour and salt and mix at low speed until just crumbly, about 15 seconds.

Pat the dough evenly into the prepared pan. Bake for 15–18 minutes, until it is lightly golden.

When the crust is done, pour the caramel evenly over it. Sprinkle on the nuts.

Cool completely in the refrigerator and store there as well, cutting into 48 bars when ready to serve.

As I have said before, the combination of salty and sweet gets me every time. Like a great candy bar, this dessert is sticky, gooey, sweet, divine, and irresistible. If your family has nut allergies, skip the nuts and make it a simple caramel bar.

pecan sandies

Status: Dairy or Parve

Prep Time: 10 minutes

Cook Time: 20 minutes

Yield: 70–80 cookies

1 cup (2 sticks) unsalted butter or margarine

¾ cup dark-brown sugar

1 large egg yolk

½ cup ground pecans

2½ cups all-purpose flour

½ cup sugar

1½ teaspoons ground cinnamon

Preheat oven to 325°F. Line 2 large cookie sheets with parchment paper. Set aside.

In the bowl of an electric stand mixer, cream the butter or margarine and the brown sugar on high speed. Add the egg yolk, pecans, and flour. Mix until combined thoroughly.

Divide the dough in half and, using parchment paper, roll each half into a long, 1- to 2-inch wide cylinder.

With a butter knife or small paring knife, thinly slice each cylinder into ¼-inch slices. Place on prepared cookie sheets.

Bake for 20 minutes. Remove the cookies from the oven.

In a small bowl, mix the sugar and cinnamon. While the cookies are still hot, roll them on both sides in the cinnamon-sugar mixture. Set on a rack to cool completely.

Some people write in to save the whales, others to save the rain forest. Jacob Plotsker, my guest at a recent tasting party, wrote an impassioned plea to save this cookie, which I had decided to omit from the book. After tweaking and re-testing these cookies, they received accolades at a later party as the perfect complement to a cup of tea.

baby apple tarts

Status: Dairy or Parve

Prep Time: 10 minutes

Cook Time: 20 minutes

Yield: 10 tarts

1 Granny Smith apple, cored, peeled, and very thinly sliced

1 McIntosh or Braeburn apple, cored, peeled, and very thinly sliced

juice from 1 lemon or 6 drops of bottled lemon juice

2 teaspoons pure vanilla extract

1 (17.5-ounce) box frozen puff-pastry dough

4 tablespoons (½ stick) unsalted butter or margarine

¼ cup dark-brown sugar

2 teaspoons ground cinnamon

2 egg yolks, beaten

¼ cup strawberry or apricot preserves

ice cream or whipped cream, dairy or parve, optional

Place the apple slices into a medium bowl. Toss with the lemon juice and vanilla.

Preheat the oven to 400°F. Line 2 large cookie sheets with parchment paper. Set aside.

Allow the puff pastry to come to room temperature so that you can open the folds without cracking them.

In a small pan, over medium-low heat, melt the butter or margarine with the brown sugar and cinnamon. Set aside.

Using a 4- or 5-inch diameter ramekin, glass, or cookie cutter, cut 5 rounds from each pastry sheet. Place on prepared cookie sheets. Brush each round with the beaten egg yolk.

Arrange the apple slices in a spiral pattern over each pastry round.

Brush with the cinnamon mixture.

Bake, uncovered for 20 minutes, until puffed and golden.

Melt the strawberry or apricot preserves in a small pan over low heat. Brush this glaze over each apple tart.

Serve warm. Can be served with whipped cream or a scoop of ice cream or parve ice cream if you wish.

Apple desserts are among my favorites. From a crisp to a pie, I have never met an apple dessert I didn't like. This shortcut recipe produces the cutest little tarts that are a snap to prepare. These are quick enough that I often whip them up for a midweek treat.

delectable dessert crepes

Status: Dairy or Parve

Prep Time: 15 minutes

Cook Time: 10 minutes

Yield: 10–12 crepes

1 cup all-purpose flour

2 large eggs

1½ cups milk, vanilla soy milk, or almond milk

2 teaspoons sugar

¼ teaspoon salt

canola oil or vegetable cooking spray

chocolate spread filling, such as the Israeli brand Hashahar or Nutella, or sliced strawberries and whipped cream

confectioner's sugar

chocolate syrup, such as Bosco or Lyons, optional

Place the flour, eggs, milk, sugar, and salt into a medium bowl. Beat with an electric stand mixer on medium-high speed until smooth. This can also be done in a blender. Allow the batter to rest for 10 minutes to allow the flour to absorb the liquids.

Lightly coat a 7- or 8-inch nonstick skillet or crepe pan with canola oil or nonstick cooking spray. Heat the pan over medium heat. Lift the pan from the stove and ladle 3–4 tablespoons of batter into the pan, tilting the pan to spread the batter evenly in a thin layer. Place the pan back on the heat and cook for 1 minute or until crepe lifts slightly around the edges and bubbles appear on the surface. Flip the crepe over and cook for 30 seconds on the other side. Crepes should be very light in color and must be done one at a time. Stack the crepes on top of each other on a platter. With your pan off the heat, re-oil the pan after each crepe.

Spread each crepe with the chocolate spread or strawberries and whipped cream. Roll the crepe up and serve 2 per plate. Top with confectioner's sugar. You can drizzle with chocolate syrup as well.

Crepes are an elegant dessert that are as easy as making pancakes once you get the hang of the art.

There is so much that you can do with crepes. You can stuff them with anything from chocolate spread, sliced bananas and berries, to blintze filling and lemon curd, the possibilities are endless. Drizzle them with maple syrup, strawberry syrup, caramel sauce, or chocolate sauce.

For a savory crepe, leave out the sugar in the recipe and in its place add an additional ½ teaspoon salt. Stuff them with vegetables, mushrooms, chicken, mashed potatoes; again, use your imagination.

To make the process smoother, it is helpful to ladle out the batter into portioned cups before you start frying. This way as soon as one crepe is done you can quickly pour in the next. This will keep you in a good groove and ensure even-sized crepes. A crepe pan is an inexpensive luxury and turns out perfect crepes. At the very least you must use a nonstick skillet; crepes stick mercilessly on stainless steel.

kettle corn

Status: Parve

Prep Time: 2 minutes

Cook Time: 10 minutes

Yield: 10 cups

3 tablespoons canola or vegetable oil

½ cup white-popcorn kernels

¼ cup sugar

1 tablespoon light corn syrup

½ teaspoon fine sea salt

Place the oil and 4 popcorn kernels into a large heavy-bottomed or nonstick pot or wok, with a lid. Turn the heat to just under medium. Cover the pot. When you hear the 4 kernels pop, you will know the oil has reached the right temperature. Open the lid, add the sugar and corn syrup and stir to dissolve. Immediately add the remaining popcorn kernels and salt. Stir. Cover the pot.

With kitchen towels or oven mitts to protect your hands, hold the lid on the pot or wok and shake continuously over the heat. Keep the contents moving or the sugar will burn and the popcorn will stick. Do not remove the lid or kernels will shoot out. Once the popping has slowed, remove from heat to prevent the sugar from scorching. Immediately transfer the kettle corn to a large bowl.

Store for up to one day in an airtight container.

Every summer our family joins our Maryland friends, the Gun family, at different amusement parks. Last summer we went to Hershey Park in Pennsylvania. While my daredevil kids rode the roller coasters, I checked out the eats! Not only do they have great kosher food, but there is a stand that sells kettle corn, a childhood favorite of mine. I love the combination of salty and sweet in snacks, and this dessert is no different. I have even tried this with Splenda sugar substitute for a sugar-free treat. It works great.

The recipe could not be easier, but follow the directions or you will end up with a burnt mess of sugar on the bottom of your pot. Select a large nonstick pot or wok with a lid. If you don't have nonstick, use a good heavy-duty pot. Keep 2 kitchen towels or potholders nearby. Your arms will get a good workout doing all that shaking, but hey, you can reward your exercise with a huge bowl of kettle corn.

caribbean rum cake

Status: Parve

Prep Time: 10 minutes

Cook Time: 1 hour

Yield: 10–12 servings

1½ cups (7-ounce bag) Butter Toffee Glazed walnuts, such as Emerald brand, or pecan halves

2 cups all-purpose flour

2 cups sugar

2 teaspoons baking powder

1 (3.4-ounce) package instant vanilla pudding, such as Jell-O brand

⅔ cup canola oil

4 large eggs

¾ cup (6-ounce can) pineapple juice

½ cup rum

Preheat oven to 350°F. Very heavily grease and flour a 10-inch tube pan; you can use the nonstick spray can with flour. The sugar in the nuts will stick if you don't grease and flour the pan enough. Sprinkle the glazed walnuts or chopped pecans on the bottom of the pan. Set aside.

In the bowl of an electric stand mixer, mix the flour, sugar, baking powder, and pudding mix. Add the oil, eggs, pineapple juice, and rum. Beat on medium-high speed until a smooth batter forms.

Pour into the prepared pan and bake for 55–60 minutes.

Allow to cool for 5 minutes. Run a knife or small offset spatula around the outside of the cake and around the tube to loosen it. With a towel to protect your hand, push the tube out from the bottom while pulling it from the top. Run the knife or spatula around the tube base to loosen to bottom of the cake from the tube base. Turn the cake out onto a plate and allow to cool.

The Butter Toffee Glazed walnuts in this dense cake are fabulous, parve, and sold in supermarkets where they sell dried fruits and nuts. If you can't find them, you can use chopped pecans.

banana-caramel cream pie

Status: Dairy or Parve

Prep Time: 10 minutes

Cook Time: none

Needs chill time

Yield: 8 servings

1 batch Thick Caramel (see page 304) or store-bought dairy caramel

1 (3.4-ounce) box instant vanilla or French vanilla pudding and pie filling, such as Jell-O brand

1¼ cups cold milk or soy milk

4 medium bananas, peeled and sliced

1 cup heavy cream or nondairy whipping cream (for parve I like Richwhip brand)

store-bought graham cracker pie crust

Prepare a batch of the Thick Caramel as directed. Set aside in refrigerator to cool while you prepare the rest of the recipe.

In a medium bowl, whisk the pudding mix with the milk for 2 minutes. Mix the banana slices into the bowl of pudding.

In the bowl of an electric stand mixer, whip the cream on high until it forms stiff peaks. Fold 3 tablespoons of the caramel into the whipped cream.

Pour the bananas and pudding into the pie crust. Top with the caramel whipped cream.

Drizzle with additional caramel, or you can serve the extra on the side.

Place into the refrigerator to cool completely. Serve chilled.

Thick, gooey caramel drizzled over mounds of bananas and cream make this no-bake dessert a dreamy delight. The store-bought graham cracker crust means it is a snap to prepare. The caramel can be skipped but is easy enough to make and does not take very long. It adds an out-of-this-world dimension to this pie that your friends and family will adore.

streusel-stuffed baked apples

Status: Dairy or Parve

Prep Time: 10 minutes

Cook Time: 30 minutes

Yield: 6 servings

¾ cup all-purpose flour

¾ cup dark-brown sugar

½ cup old-fashioned rolled oats (not quick cooking or 1-minute type)

6 tablespoons (¾ stick) unsalted butter or margarine, melted

3 medium red apples, such as McIntosh or Cortland

3 medium green apples, such as Granny Smith

1 cup apple juice

½ cup honey

2 teaspoons ground cinnamon

Thick Caramel (see page 304), optional

ice cream or whipped cream, dairy or parve, optional

Preheat oven to 425°F.

Prepare the streusel filling: In a medium bowl, combine the flour, brown sugar, oats, and melted butter or margarine. Pinch to form coarse crumbs. Set aside.

Wash the apples and, with a melon baller, carefully scoop out the core, creating a "bowl" about 2 inches in diameter. Be careful not to go all the way to the bottom or to break the sides.

Fill each apple with the streusel filling, stuffing them to their tops.

Arrange the apples in a shallow 9- by 9-inch baking dish.

In a small bowl, stir the apple juice, honey, and cinnamon. Pour into the baking pan.

Bake, uncovered, for 25–30 minutes or until the apples are tender. If the streusel starts to burn, loosely cover with a piece of foil.

Carefully remove the apples to a platter or individual dessert dishes.

Drizzle the apples with the pan juices or the Thick Caramel and serve warm with a scoop of your favorite ice cream or whipped cream.

All the beauty and flavor of an apple pie without the labor and calories of the crust!

chocolate pull-apart babka

Status: Dairy or Parve

Prep Time: 20 minutes

Cook Time: 40 minutes

Yield: 6 servings

1 (14-ounce) box frozen challah-roll dough, such as Kineret brand Chall-Ettes

3 tablespoon good-quality Dutch process cocoa powder, such as Droste brand

½ cup sugar

2 tablespoons all-purpose flour

1 tablespoon pure vanilla extract

5 tablespoons unsalted butter or margarine, melted

Preheat oven to 325°F. Cut a sheet of parchment paper to fit the bottom and up the sides of a 5½- by 10½-inch loaf pan, or spray heavily with nonstick cooking spray. The parchment paper will enable you to remove the babka from the pan and transfer it to a serving tray; without it, you may need to serve it from the loaf pan.

Open the packaging of the challah-roll dough. Allow the challah rolls to stand at room temperature for 10–15 minutes, until the rolls are soft enough to un-knot.

In a medium bowl, mix the cocoa powder, sugar, flour, and vanilla. Stir to combine.

Break each strand of challah dough into 5–6 pieces. Roll each piece into a ball between your palms. Drop the balls a few at a time into the cocoa mixture. Dip each ball into the melted butter or margarine, shake off excess, and then drop back into the cocoa mixture. Drop into the prepared pan.

Pour the remaining cocoa mixture into the remaining butter or margarine and use your fingers to pinch it into coarse crumbs. Sprinkle over the top of the babka.

Cover the pan with a kitchen towel. Open the door of the preheated oven and set the pan on the open door. The indirect heat from the oven will help it rise quickly. Allow to sit for 15 minutes. Alternatively, microwave 2 cups of water until boiling, about 5 minutes. Quickly remove the measuring cup and place the babka into the microwave. Allow it to rest in the warm, steamy, microwave for 15 minutes.

Close the oven door, or remove the babka from the microwave, and allow the oven to return 325°F. Bake the babka for 20–25 minutes.

Serve warm. To remove the babka from the loaf pan, slip a spatula under the parchment. Hold a platter over the pan and flip the cake out. Carefully flip it back over so that the chocolate crumbs face up.

A few years ago, I was looking for a recipe tester. I immediately thought of my friend Limor Decter, who is a fabulous cook and entertainer. She was not interested in the job but thought she might know someone for me. Ten minutes later she called, laughing, and said, "I called my friend Paula Shoyer, working woman, mother of 4, and on this beautiful sunny day she was relaxing at home making babka from scratch!" Limor knew this was the woman for my job. I don't know many people who take the time to make babka from scratch. I also don't know many people who don't like chocolate babka, so here is my solution. It is wonderful right out of the oven, but when that is not possible, at least re-warm it for a few minutes before serving.

orange-coconut cake

Status: Dairy or Parve
Prep Time: 10 minutes
Cook Time: 55 minutes
Yield: 16 servings

3 cups all-purpose flour

2 cups sugar

1 tablespoon baking powder

½ teaspoon fine sea salt

1 cup canola or vegetable oil

1 cup orange juice, not from concentrate

1 teaspoon pure vanilla extract

4 large eggs

zest of 1 orange

COCONUT CRUNCH:

1 cup all-purpose flour

½ cup dark-brown sugar

½ cup sweetened flaked coconut

6 tablespoons (¾ stick) unsalted butter or margarine, melted

GLAZE:

3 cups confectioner's sugar

4½ tablespoons orange juice or less

1 cup sweetened flaked coconut

Preheat oven to 350°F. Heavily grease and flour a 12-cup fluted bundt pan or tube pan. You can use the cooking spray that has both oil and flour in it.

In a medium bowl, whisk the flour, sugar, baking powder, and salt.

In the bowl of a stand mixer, at medium speed, beat the oil, orange juice, vanilla, eggs, and orange zest until smooth. Blend in the flour mixture. Mix for 2 minutes on medium speed. Set aside.

Prepare the coconut crunch: In a medium bowl, combine the flour, brown sugar, coconut, and melted margarine. Use your fingertips to pinch into coarse crumbs.

Pour half the cake batter into prepared pan. Top with half the coconut crunch. Top with remaining cake batter. Sprinkle remaining crunch on top.

Bake for 55 minutes, or until a toothpick inserted into the center comes out clean. Allow the cake to cool for 5 minutes. Turn the cake out onto a rack to cool completely.

Prepare the glaze: In a small bowl, mix the confectioner's sugar and 2 tablespoons orange juice. Stir vigorously; it will get easier to mix. You should add as little liquid as possible so that the glaze is thick and dark. Add remaining orange juice, as needed, to make a thick but pourable glaze. Spoon over the cake. Immediately sprinkle on flaked coconut, pressing it lightly into the sides.

This heavenly-looking cake, covered in glaze and drenched with coconut, is moist and full of flavor. The nut layer adds a nice crunch and the cake is sturdy enough to travel well.

warm runny chocolate soufflés

Status: Dairy or Parve

Prep Time: 10 minutes

Cook Time: 15 minutes

Yield: 8 servings

4 ounces good-quality semi-sweet or bittersweet chocolate, such as Noblesse

½ cup (1 stick) unsalted butter or margarine

4 large eggs

1½ cups sugar, plus more for coating ramekins

¾ cup all-purpose flour

1 teaspoon pure vanilla extract

Preheat oven to 450°F. Generously coat 8 (6.8-ounce) ramekins with nonstick cooking spray, and lightly coat them with granulated sugar. Hold a ramekin on its side. Tap the sides, turning the ramekin to coat the sides with sugar as well. Repeat with remaining ramekins. (If you use larger ramekins you will get fewer servings.)

Break the chocolate into small pieces; place it and the butter or margarine in a small microwave-safe dish. Microwave on medium power for 15-second intervals, stirring between, until the chocolate is completely melted.

In the bowl of an electric stand mixer, beat the eggs on high speed until foamy. Slowly pour in the sugar, and continue beating until very fluffy and pale yellow. On low speed, stir in the flour and vanilla, until thoroughly combined.

Increase speed to high, and while beating, slowly drizzle in the melted chocolate mixture. Once added, beat until all the chocolate is incorporated, about 1 minute.

For ease of pouring, transfer the batter into a large measuring cup. Fill each ramekin halfway. Set the ramekins onto a baking sheet, and bake for 14–15 minutes until the tops are brown and the centers are warm.

(Alternatively, the filled ramekins can be refrigerated. Just leave at room temperature for 30 minutes before baking.)

Serve immediately, being cautious as the ramekins will be hot!

Molten chocolate cakes have made a huge splash in restaurants in recent years. I love the idea but I am not always thrilled with the taste or texture. Even after playing around and trying to develop a recipe for this book, I was not satisfied. When I was about to give up, my food guru and food stylist, Melanie Dubberley, suggested I try using my favorite brownie recipe and just undercook it. I turned to Fishbein Brownies, in our family for generations, beloved by literally hundreds of eaters, and gave the theory a try. Less a molten cake, more of a soufflé, call it what you want, it was spectacular. Here was the chocolate flavor I was looking for and the warm runny center that is the signature of this dessert.

french almond macaroons

Status: Parve

Prep Time: 10 minutes

Cook Time: 20 minutes

Yield: 24 cookies

2¼ cups confectioner's sugar

1 cup blanched slivered almonds

¼ cup all-purpose flour

3 large egg whites

pinch sea salt

Preheat the oven to 400°F. Line 2 large cookie sheets with parchment paper.

Place the confectioner's sugar and almonds into the bowl of a food processor fitted with a metal blade. Process for a full 3 minutes so that the almonds are ground to a powder. Add the flour and process for 1 minute more. Transfer the almond mixture to a medium bowl. Set aside.

Place the egg whites and salt into the bowl of a stand mixer. Beat on high speed until stiff peaks form.

With a spatula, fold the almond mixture into the egg whites in three parts, using the spatula to fold the egg whites over and over until the almond mixture is incorporated. The batter will be sticky and thick.

Spoon the batter by full tablespoons onto the prepared sheets, leaving room for the macaroons to spread as they bake.

Bake 1 sheet at a time for 8–10 minutes or until the cookie are puffed, shiny, and have formed a skin on top.

When the cookies come out of the oven, slide the parchment paper off the hot sheet and allow to cool completely before removing the cookies.

Although I'm a big fan of the can, macaroons mean different things to different people. Yes, the can on Passover means mounds of chewy coconut that I do look forward to. However, there is nothing like a French macaroon. These contain no coconut. Instead they are soft pillows of almond and meringue. Made right, they are the perfect balance between sticky and chewy and are sold at every patisserie in Paris dressed up in many ways. You can flavor them with liqueurs, sandwich jelly or chocolate ganache between two cookies, or just drizzle chocolate over the tops. Personally I love them plain. The recipe is simple; just make sure you whip the egg whites properly so they are stiff but not dry. If your stand mixer has a whisk attachment you should use it. You must use parchment paper to line the cookie sheet or your cookies will stick miserably.

no-bake giant napoleon cake

Status: Dairy or Parve

Prep Time: 15 minutes

Cook Time: none

Needs chill time

Yield: 12 servings

butter or margarine, for greasing

2 (3.4-ounce) boxes instant vanilla pudding & pie filling

2½ cups milk or soy milk

1 cup heavy cream or nondairy whipping cream (for parve I like Richwhip brand)

1 box honey-graham crackers

3 ounces good-quality semi-sweet chocolate, such as Scharffen Berger, broken into ½-inch pieces

⅔ cup honey, such as Golden Blossom

With butter or margarine, lightly grease a 9- by 13-inch baking pan. Set aside.

In a medium bowl, whisk the pudding mix with milk until thoroughly blended.

In the bowl of a stand mixer, on medium-high speed, beat the whipping cream until thick and stiff peaks form, about 5 minutes.

Fold the whipped cream into the pudding mixture.

Arrange a single layer of graham crackers in the prepared pan. Top with half the pudding mixture. Use an offset spatula to spread evenly over the graham crackers.

Top with a second layer of graham crackers. Add the remaining pudding, spreading with the offset spatula. Top with a layer of graham crackers.

Place the chopped chocolate and honey into a microwave-safe bowl. Microwave on high power for 30 seconds. Stir until smooth and melted.

Pour the glaze over the top layer of graham crackers. Use the offset spatula to spread evenly.

Place into the refrigerator, uncovered, or without allowing the cover to touch the chocolate. Allow to fully chill and set. This can be made a day or two in advance.

My mom used to make this all the time when I was growing up. For awhile, it became hard to find good-quality kosher instant pudding. Recently the Jell-O company made their puddings kosher and my family is back in business! This couldn't be easier and, since there is no baking involved, it is simple enough for a child to make. When I make this a Chocolate Chocolate Napoleon cake I use the Jell-O brand Devil's Food Flavor Instant Pudding and Pie Filling, mix it with 3 cups of milk or soymilk, and follow the directions as above.

chocolate-drenched stuffed fruit

Status: Parve

Prep Time: 20 minutes

Cook Time: none

Needs chill time

Yield: 6 servings

4 (3.5oz) bars good-quality parve bittersweet Swiss chocolate, such as Noblesse

12 large raspberries

1 tablespoon sweetened, shredded coconut, divided

12 medium-large strawberries

12 large blueberries

2 medium bananas

12 pecan halves

Line a large cookie sheet with parchment paper. Place a small cooling rack on a small cookie sheet.

Stuff the raspberries with about ¼ teaspoon of coconut, and place them on the cooling rack, coconut side up.

Remove the greens and dig a hole about the size of a blueberry in the tops of the strawberries. Gently press a blueberry to fit deep into each prepared strawberry. Place these on one side of the parchment-lined cookie sheet.

Peel each banana and slice it on the bias into 6 pieces. Place the banana bites on the other side of the parchment-lined cookie sheet.

Fill a medium pot with 2–3 inches of water. Over medium-low heat, bring the water to just simmering (about 175–180°F). Using a serrated knife, chop the chocolate into ½-inch pieces. Reserve about ¼ of the chopped chocolate away from the heat. Place the remaining three-quarters of the chocolate (about 10 ounces) into a large metal bowl and set the bowl over the barely simmering water.

Using a wooden spoon, slowly stir the chocolate often until it is melted, scraping down the sides of the bowl as needed. Do NOT let the water come to a rolling simmer or boil; excessive heat will damage the chocolate. Once all the chocolate is melted, immediately remove the bowl from the heat and add the remaining chopped chocolate. Gently stir until all the chocolate is melted.

Working quickly, drop a banana piece into the chocolate. Without stabbing it, lift it out of the chocolate with a fork. Lightly tap the back of the fork on the edge of the bowl, and then slide it over the edge to remove any excess chocolate. Place the banana back on parchment lined cookie sheet. Top with a pecan. Repeat with the remaining pieces.

With a firm but gentle grip on the point of a strawberry, dip it about ¾ of the way up, being careful not to lose the blueberry. Place the berry back on the parchment-lined cookie sheet, blueberry side down. Repeat with remaining strawberries.

Using a small spoon, gently drizzle the remaining chocolate over the prepared raspberries.

Place all fruit in the refrigerator; serve well chilled. Eat within a couple of hours. Or store in a air-tight container refrigerated for one day or in the freezer for up to a week. They are great frozen treats!

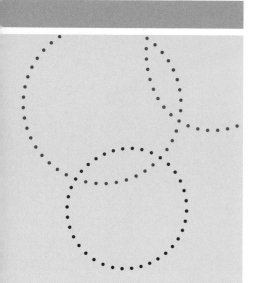

The recipes in this section are what I consider "building block" recipes. Each recipe is for an ingredient that, when prepared once, can be used in dozens of ways and in a variety of recipes. Although none is difficult, some of them take a little time to make. Spend a little time on a Sunday night roasting tomatoes or caramelizing onions and you will be rewarded with a great ingredient that can turn a few simple week-night dishes into four-star meals.

These ingredients are perfect to have on hand for the times when you are not working from a recipe and need to improvise with what you have. When you are tossing together a little of this and a little of that, adding any of these ingredients will take your results to another dimension.

Each recipe can be doubled or tripled, as it takes very little extra work or time to make a larger batch, and each ingredient can last for days in the refrigerator. Think through, in advance, how you could use an ingredient in a few ways within a week. Included in each recipe you will find a list of suggestions on ways to use it. Roasted garlic, for example, is a favorite of mine. I love serving a whole head of roasted garlic at each person's place setting on Friday night to smear over challah. I spread it over the skin of a whole chicken before roasting, or squeeze over fish before baking it. I add roasted garlic to salad dressings and to sauces. The possibilities are endless if you have the prepared ingredients on hand.

BUILDING BLOCK RECIPES

croutons

Status: Parve

Prep Time: 5 minutes

Cook Time: 15 minutes

2 (12-inch) French baguettes or loaves of Italian or sourdough bread, crusts removed

⅓ cup olive oil

3 cloves fresh garlic, minced

1 teaspoon dried thyme, dried rosemary, or dried oregano, or a combination of these, optional

fine sea salt

freshly ground black pepper

Preheat the oven to 350°F. Line a baking sheet with parchment paper. Set aside.

Slice the bread into 1-inch slices. Cut each slice into ¾-inch cubes. You should have about 4–5 cups of cubes. Place the bread cubes into a large mixing bowl.

Mix the olive oil with the minced garlic and any herbs, if desired. Drizzle the oil over the cubes and toss them. You want the cubes to be coated but not saturated or your croutons will be too oily. Sprinkle with salt and pepper. Place in a single layer on the prepared baking sheet. Bake for 12–14 minutes, tossing with a spatula halfway through the baking time, until toasted and golden.

SUGGESTED USES

- garnish for salad
- garnish for soup
- add to soup to thicken it
- make fresh bread crumbs
- for stuffing

oven-dried tomatoes

Status: Parve

Prep Time: 10 minutes

Cook Time: 4–5 hours

10 ripe plum tomatoes

4 cloves fresh garlic, minced

olive oil

coarse sea salt

Preheat oven to 250°F. Line a large jelly roll pan with parchment paper. Set a metal cooling rack in the pan.

Cut each tomato in half lengthwise. With the back of a spoon or a melon baller, scoop out and discard the seeds and juice.

Place the scooped-out tomato halves into a large bowl. Toss with the minced garlic and oil. Sprinkle with a large pinch of salt.

Place the tomatoes cut-side-down on the prepared rack. Place them into the oven and allow them to dry for 4–5 hours. (If you do not have a rack you will need to turn the tomatoes after the first 2 hours to keep them from steaming.) They should be dried but not leathery.

Transfer the tomatoes to a container and cover. They will keep for 1 week in the refrigerator.

SUGGESTED USES

- slice into salads
- process in the food processor to make a paste to spread on chicken or fish
- add to pasta dishes
- add to risotto
- chop with basil and minced garlic for bruschetta
- use on an antipasto platter
- slice into an omelete or fritatta
- serve with cheese

pesto

2 cups (8 ounces leaves and stems) firmly packed fresh basil leaves, washed and dried

1 clove fresh garlic

3 tablespoons pine nuts

⅓ cup Parmesan cheese, optional for dairy meals

½ cup extra-virgin olive oil, plus more if needed

⅛ teaspoon fine sea salt

Place the basil leaves in the bowl of a food processor fitted with a metal blade. Pulse until coarsely chopped. Add the garlic and nuts. Add cheese, if using. Pulse 5–6 times. With the machine running, drizzle in ½ cup olive oil. Stop to scrape down the sides of the container. Add the salt. Process to form a thick paste.

Transfer to a container. If not using immediately, top the pesto with ¼-inch of extra-virgin olive oil and cover the container. Before using, pour off this layer of olive oil. The pesto will keep in the refrigerator for one week.

SUGGESTED USES

- toss with green beans
- spread over chicken, steak, or lamb
- stir into hot soup as a garnish
- serve with fresh fish
- add as a layer to lasagne
- spread on tuna or other sandwich

- serve with brie and tomatoes
- spread with fresh mozzarella
- toss with pasta and a little of the cooking water
- spread over lightly toasted French bread slices

caramelized onions

Status: Parve

Prep Time: 10 minutes

Cook Time: 35 minutes

5 medium Vidalia or other sweet onions

1½ tablespoons olive oil

fine sea salt

freshly ground black pepper

Cut each onion in half from the root end to the stem end. Peel the halves. Place each half cut-side-down on a work surface. Trim off the ends and thinly slice the onion from the root end to the stem end. This will keep the onions more intact as they caramelize and keep them from becoming a mush.

Heat the olive oil in a large skillet over low heat. Add the sliced onions. Cook, uncovered, for 30–35 minutes, stirring frequently, until the onions are soft and golden-brown. Season with salt and pepper.

If not using right away, transfer to a container. The onions will keep for one week in the refrigerator or can be frozen.

SUGGESTED USES

- add to egg salad
- stir into gravy
- scatter over steak
- use as a topping for pizza
- bake into challah dough
- arrange over chicken cutlets
- add to rice pilaf
- cook into omelets or fritatta
- serve as a topping for hamburgers
- mix into mashed potatoes
- scatter over steamed cauliflower

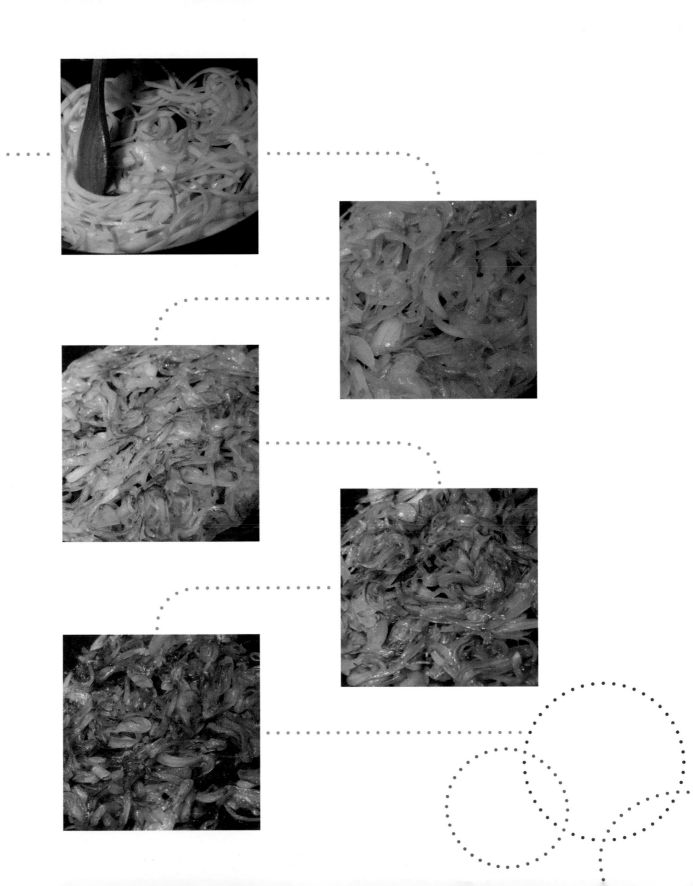

roasted garlic

Status: Parve

Prep Time: 5 minutes

Cook Time: 1 hour

4-5 whole heads of garlic

olive oil

fine sea salt

Preheat oven to 375°F. Prepare 4 to 5 squares of foil. Have a small baking pan ready.

Holding the head of garlic on its side, cut the top 1–2 inches off the top of the bulb to expose the cloves. Place the head in the center of a square of foil. Drizzle with olive oil and season with salt. Close the foil packet and place into a baking pan. Repeat with remaining heads. Roast for 1 hour or until garlic is caramelized and easily squeezes like a paste from the head.

Keep the heads in the foil and in a Ziploc bag in the refrigerator for 4–5 days.

Re-warm or bring back to room temperature before serving.

SUGGESTED USES

- add to mayonnaise as a topping for hamburgers, grilled eggplant, or grilled tuna
- add to pasta or pasta sauces
- add to salad dressings
- squeeze into mashed potatoes
- spread on a baguette to make garlic bread
- spread on chicken or fish
- serve small heads to spread on challah

Kosher by Design Short on Time

thick caramel

Status: Parve

Prep Time: 5 minutes

Cook Time: 15 minutes

½ teaspoon good-quality Dutch-process cocoa powder, such as Droste brand

⅔ cup nondairy whipping cream, such as Richwhip brand

1 cup light corn syrup

½ cup water

3 cups sugar

1½ teaspoons lime juice

1 tablespoon margarine

¾ teaspoon pure vanilla extract

In a medium bowl, whisk the cocoa powder in the whipping cream until cocoa powder is completely dissolved, smoothing out any lumps. Add the corn syrup, whisk again, and set aside.

In a medium heavy-bottomed pot, combine the ½ cup water, sugar, and lime juice. Over medium-high heat, bring the mixture to a boil, stirring constantly until the sugar dissolves. With a pastry brush soaked in water, brush the sides of the pot clean to remove splatters. Cook without stirring. As the water evaporates, the bubbles will become bigger and slower; start watching for the caramel color to appear. Swirl or turn the pot to avoid getting a burned spot and to evenly mix the syrup. Simmer until the mixture is an amber color. Go by the color, as the heat will differ from stove to stove. Don't allow the caramel to burn and work carefully so as not to burn yourself.

Whisk in the whipping cream mixture. The caramel will bubble profusely and may clump. Keep stirring until the caramel is smooth in color and texture. Simmer for 2–3 minutes or until slightly thickened. Remove from heat and stir in the margarine and the vanilla.

The caramel will be extremely hot, so exercise caution as you carefully transfer to a large bowl and place into the refrigerator. The caramel will thicken as it cools. To use as a topping, re-heat in the microwave until syrupy.

SUGGESTED USES

- drizzle over ice cream
- swirl into warm Rice-Krispie Treat batter
- use as a dip for apple or pear slices
- use as a topping for a plain cheesecake
- in Caramel Nut Bars, see page 264
- in Banana-Caramel Cream Pie, see page 276
- in Streusel-Stuffed Baked Apples, see page 278

caramelized nuts

Status: Parve

Prep Time: 5 minutes

Cook Time: 15 minutes

8 ounces unsalted nuts, such as almonds, pecans, walnut halves, cashews, or any combination

½ cup sugar

¼ cup water

1½ tablespoons honey

Preheat oven to 350°F. Line two baking sheets with parchment paper and spray with nonstick cooking spray.

Place the nuts into a large bowl.

Bring the sugar, water, and honey to a boil in a small pot over medium heat. Stir the mixture until the sugar is dissolved.

Pour the sugar mixture over the nuts and stir until well coated.

Transfer the nuts with a fork or slotted spoon onto one of the prepared baking sheets, and arrange in a single layer, leaving the syrup in the bowl.

Bake for 10–12 minutes, until the nuts are caramelized and golden. If you want them to look smooth and shiny, do not stir them. If you want them to look caramelized and candied, toss them with a greased slotted spatula halfway through the baking time. Spread the nuts on the second prepared baking sheet, separate any clusters, and cool completely.

Store for one week in an airtight container.

SUGGESTED USES

- serve as a snack
- sprinkle over salads
- sprinkle over ice cream
- roll into pastry

- serve with brie or other cheeses
- serve chopped over pear slices
- mix into yogurt
- garnish a cake

QUICK & EASY

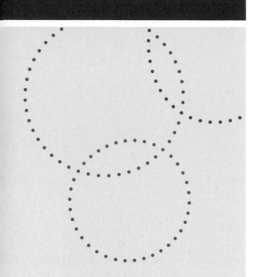

I love a great tablescape, fabulous floral centerpieces, and all the touches that make a dinner or lunch party feel extraordinary. While it's true that the food itself matters most, the setting also plays a part in our enjoyment of a meal, whether it's fancy or casual, planned long in advance or put together on the spur of the moment. Whatever the occasion, table décor sets the mood and makes your guests feel that they're part of something special.

For some parties, you start planning long in advance, carefully choreographing every detail from the centerpieces to the toothpicks. Sometimes, however, entertaining can be a last-minute thing. And sometimes even parties that are long in the making can just sneak up on you. This does not mean that you cannot have a memorable event. Just the smallest touches can make even paper plates look special.

My creative team, Renée Erreich and Larry Sexton, and I have filled this section with great ideas that are meant to serve as inspiration. Take a look around your home at the things you already own. Look at them in a new way; you might have just the perfect item or group of items to help you design a quick and easy centerpiece or tablescape. And when designing your table, think color, of course, but also shape, texture, and height. To get you started, I have divided the ideas into four categories:

USING WHAT YOU HAVE. Starting with the assumption that most of us have attractive, interesting collections—ceramics, glassware, art objects, folk art, or what-have-you—we took things that were all in different places in my home and grouped them together for impact or to form a design.

CLOSET RE-USABLES: A stash of materials that I keep tucked away in a closet and can pull out at a moment's notice for a sensational arrangement.

KIDS' CENTERPIECES: Grown-ups and kids alike will love these simple and edible centerpieces that can turn any meal into an event.

TABLE DÉCOR

SIMPLE FLORAL IDEAS: Whether it be time or budget, not every event calls for an elaborate centerpiece or expensive call to the florist. Sometimes it can be plucked right from your own backyard or even put together from what you can buy for a minimal amount of money. By arranging the flowers artfully you get huge bang for your buck.

Don't feel that you've got enough stuff? Over the years, I've gotten into the habit of shopping with table décor in mind. Thrift stores and tag sales are great sources of fantastic things that don't cost much. Look for lacy table linens, colorful picnic cloths (to transform your dining room table into a campground), and other textiles (baby blankets make great tablecloths for baby showers). Pick up mismatched silverware and crockery (don't pass up odd pieces; mix 'n match items can make for a lovely, conversation-starting table if you think in terms of themes and color schemes). For a more whimsical approach, pick up small items such as toys (imagine a table decorated with toy cars or trains—or alternatively, with rag dolls or dozens of beaded necklaces), sports stuff (baseball cards, caps, helmets, balls), music (how 'bout a centerpiece with a base made from an old LP?)

Small ethnic markets can also be a source of table props. Asian stores often sell inexpensive porcelain pieces, chopsticks, and other trinkets. A Mexican market might offer colorful ceramics. You never know what you may find. That's true when you travel, too. If you've had your fill of T-shirts from exotic locales, think table décor when you browse through souvenir shops on your next trip.

And don't forget your local supermarket. Some of the most sumptuous tablescapes are made of items you can buy in the produce and grocery aisles. Large trays of colorful dried beans can make an evocative base for smaller serving platters on a buffet. Seasonal fruits and veggies are easily transformed into eye-popping centerpieces. (Picture a big basket of tomatoes and eggplants in summer, or polished apples in the fall). Your imagination is the only limit!

using what you have

About 10 years ago, inspired by my mom and aunt, I started collecting figural teapots. I have close to 100 teapots of all shapes and sizes. Some are antique; some are just plain fun. Grouping them as a runner down the center of my table, adds height and color. They are real conversation pieces, as each teapot comes with a story of how and when I came to acquire it. Whether you collect salt and pepper shakers, colored glass, postcards, or model cars, anything that is part of you will create immediate interest, and, when grouped together, can have great visual appeal.

Even your clothing closet can serve as inspiration when designing a table. Here we show an assortment of scarves that overlap each other to form a tablecloth. The vibrant colors add real elegance.

using what you have

using what you have

By stacking footed cake plates and playing with flower heads you can achieve a very beautiful centerpiece/ food display. Don't just save this idea for dessert. Hors d'oeuvres or side dishes will look just as great. Be sure any flowers you place on food are both edible and have not been treated with pesticide or other chemicals.

using what you have

On many happy occasions throughout the years of my marriage, I have received many wonderful floral arrangements. Long after the flowers have died, I am left with vases of various shapes and heights. By grouping them together with some glass salad bowls we have formed a great food display. I set up the meal up buffet style and used the vases as containers. They are clear, so the beauty of the food shows through. You can even use the taller, thinner vases to hold drinks; so much more elegant than a bottle of soda or container of juice. The smallest vases can be used to hold dressings or sauces.

closet re-useables

This simple centerpiece will thrill your guests and leave them awestruck. Collect large branches or make a one-time purchase of curly willow at a garden center or florist. Long ribbons are simply tied to the branches that are placed into a tall, thin vase. You can change the color scheme by changing the ribbons or simply leave the ribbons on the branches and change the rest of the table. To coordinate the table with the centerpiece, tie extra ribbon around each napkin.

closet re-useables

I have a few crystal candlesticks in my living room. By placing colored glass votive holders in them and scattering some pink glass beads at the base, I have a stunning centerpiece that shines from top to bottom.

closet re-useables

What could be more fun than feathers? Feathers are an inexpensive one-time crafts store purchase that can be saved and re-used dozens of times. Stand some in tall, skinny vases and scatter others on the table around the base of the vases. The white feathers give an ethereal look, but you can go for whimsy and try a splash of color as well. When your party is done, gather the feathers, put a rubber band around them, and stash them away until your next shindig.

closet re-useables

From years of trips to the beach with my kids and a few backyard beach parties, we have an impressive collection of shells. On a natural-looking tablecloth, we put clear glasses filled with shells of all shapes and sizes. Twisted branches fill the space and then water is poured into each glass. Some of our larger shells are arranged in the center of the table. Starfish purchased from a crafts store or the Internet finish the look, which is perfect for a summer party or outdoor entertaining.

kids centerpieces

The key to a good kids' centerpiece is to make it large, colorful, and whimsical. These galvanized buckets filled with sugar have gorgeous lollipops stuck in them. The lollipops double as party favors at the end of a festive celebration.

kids centerpieces

Don't just wait for a birthday party to make a child feel special; in fact, have them use their toys to help you create something fabulous. Here we show Legos used as food containers. Instead of telling your kids to clean up their rooms or the basement, encourage them to create something cool.

simple floral centerpieces

Bring some tall bottles together for this simple floral idea. You can even try Coke bottles or empty wine bottles. Stick a few beautiful single stems in each for a great look.

simple floral centerpieces

This sweet look could not be easier. We filled drinking glasses with water and hydrangeas. Select a flower that gives good coverage so you don't see the glass. Stand each glass in a paper lunch bag. Fold a cuff over at the top of the bag and tie with a pretty ribbon. Make a single arrangement or many that can be grouped in a circle in the center of the table.

simple floral centerpieces

This idea was inspired by nature. We laid out a piece of moss and scattered it with artichokes, potatoes, mushrooms, leaves, and branches. We used Funtak to get the mushrooms to stand and lie the way we wanted them. Oil votives, the final touch, are interspersed with the veggies to illuminate the greenery.

simple floral centerpieces

A rock garden makes a great centerpiece. It is visually calming. Set a copper or galvanized tray in the center of your table. Lay rocks in the bottom. Don't make it too heavy or you will have a hard time moving it after the meal. Stick a few stems of a flower, such as gerbera daisies, into a piece of floral foam and set that into the corner of the tray. Cover the rocks with water.

INDEX

C

D

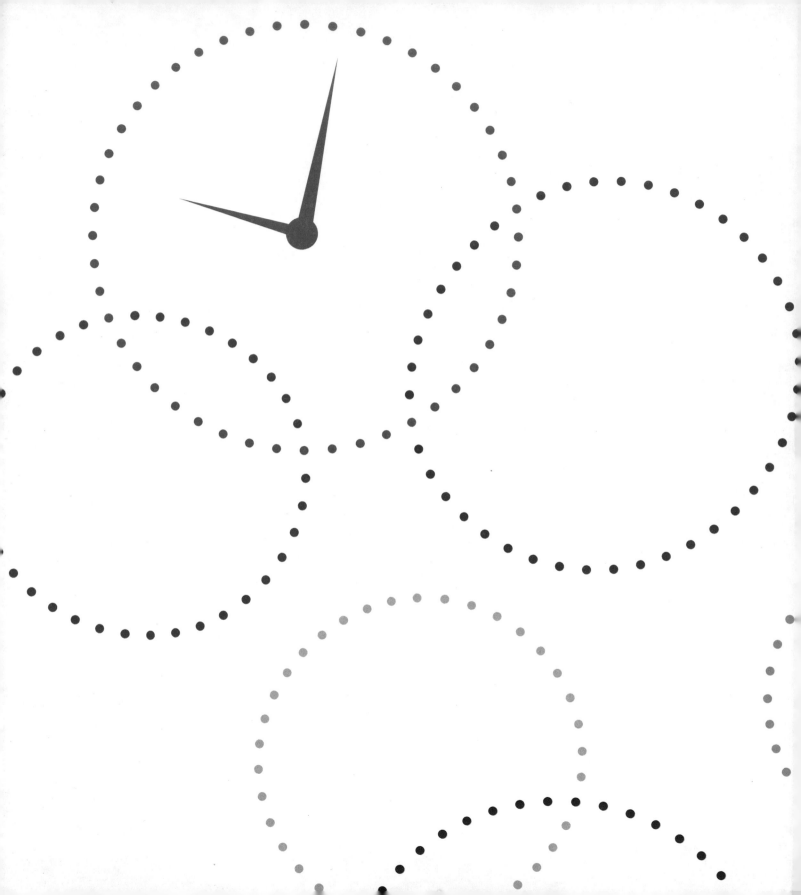